12 STEPS
TO BECOMING A
MORE ORGANIZED
WOMAN

12 STEPS
TO BECOMING A
MORE ORGANIZED
WOMAN

Practical Tips for Managing
Your Home and Your Life
Based on Proverbs 31

LANE P. JORDAN

HENDRICKSON PUBLISHERS

CONTENTS

DEDICATION

*T*HIS BOOK IS first dedicated to my daughter Christi who tirelessly taught me how to use the computer so that I could write this book. She edited every chapter and gave me unending love, support and encouragement.

To my second daughter, Grace, who is always saying "You can do it!"

To my unbelievable husband, Larry, who constantly encourages me, supports me, and helps me any way he can, in all the different things I am attempting to do at one time. You will never know how much I need you and rely on you for your wisdom and strength of character.

ACKNOWLEDGEMENTS

*I*T TAKES A surprising number of people to make a book. This one exists because of all the friends and professionals who supported and helped me. I offer heartfelt thanks:

To Peggy Anderson, who is the very best editor. Thank you for all your time, effort and encouragement in making this book flow and read so well. I am thankful for the opportunity to have worked with you.

To Scott Pinzon and Heather Stroobosscher, who fine-tuned my grammar and whose edits are appreciated more than I can express.

To Dan Penwell, who had the faith in this book to publish it. Thanks for being there for me as the publishing process went along.

To my very special friend, Marianne Vick, who encouraged me to write this book, and to the other friends who promised to pray me through it: Lynn, Shan, Lossie, Kim, Lynne, Cathy, Judy, Carol, Jan, Sandy, Diane, Jill, Cindy, Karen, Kathy, Sharon, Rachel, and my Bible Study. To all of you, thank you so much. You are true gifts from our Lord.

"Many are the plans in a man's heart, but it is the Lord's purpose that prevails" (Prov.19:21). Thank you, God, for seeing this come to pass.

PROVERBS 31:10–31

A N EXCELLENT WIFE, who can find?
 For her worth is far above jewels.
The heart of her husband trusts in her,
 And he will have no lack of gain.
She does him good and not evil
 All the days of her life.
She looks for wool and flax
 And works with her hands in delight.
She is like merchant ships;
 She brings her food from afar.
She rises also while it is still night
 And gives food to her household
 And portions to her maidens.
She considers a field and buys it;
 From her earnings she plants a vineyard.
She girds herself with strength
 And makes her arms strong.
She senses that her gain is good;
 Her lamp does not go out at night.

She stretches out her hand to the distaff,
　　And her hands grasp the spindle.
She extends her hand to the poor,
　　And stretches out her hands to the needy.
She is not afraid of the snow for her household,
　　For all her household are clothed with scarlet.
She makes coverings for herself;
　　Her clothing is fine linen and purple.
Her husband is known in the gates,
　　When he sits among the elders of the land.
She makes linen garments and sells *them,*
　　And supplies belts to the tradesmen.
Strength and dignity are her clothing,
　　And she smiles at the future.
She opens her mouth in wisdom,
　　And the teaching of kindness is on her tongue.
She looks well to the ways of her household,
　　and does not eat the bread of idleness.
Her children rise up and blessed her;
　　Her husband *also,* and he praises her, *saying:*
"Many daughters have done nobly,
　　But you excel them all."
Charm is deceitful and beauty is vain,
　　But a woman who fears the LORD, she shall be praised.
Give her the product of her hands,
　　And let her works praise her in the gates.

INTRODUCTION

*W*ELL, WE MUST BE pretty ambitious, you and I. You because you picked up this book and me because I wanted to write it. It would be nice if this book were like a magic wand, that by merely holding it, we could instantly become more organized. Obviously, it's not, but all is not lost. Anyone who wants to become more organized can.

I believe in a God who truly cares about every detail in our lives. A God who wants our lives to be rich and full and complete. He cares when a new mother needs sleep because she was up all night with a little one. He cares when a marriage is on the rocks. He cares when we have to juggle our home life with our work. He knows what it's like to be hungry and not have the energy to buy or cook food. He cares how we feel and he cares how we live the life he gave us.

He wants to give us "life abundantly." He says so in John 10:10: "The thief comes only to steal and kill and destroy; I came that they might have life, and have it abundantly." By studying his words and his ways, we can pull our lives together so that they will be a blessing to us and to others, and a glory to our Lord. It just takes the right motivation and a gentle push into being more organized.

Each person has been created by God to be a unique individual. We each have different talents and abilities. Some people are orderly by nature while others are not. Since I was a little girl, I've liked to put things in order. I remember calling my mother into my room to show her how neatly I had stacked all the shoes in my closet. I was so proud of that accomplishment and so glad she didn't tease me about it. She must have known I'd rather straighten my doll's clothes than actually play with them.

I learned early that there was value in being organized. When I was about ten years old, I went on an overnight camping trip. It felt so good to be in the country and to nestle down deep into my sleeping bag. The next morning, however, the counselors were covering everyone's heads. It had begun to pour rain and they were trying to let us sleep a little longer, by keeping us dry. All my stuff was wet and messy. I couldn't find dry socks, or anything else I needed to feel more like a person than like a wet duck. How I wished I'd put my belongings neatly away the night before, so they'd be safe and dry. In that moment, I first understood why it was good to be organized.

That incident proved to be a blessing in my life because it showed me that keeping things in order had an ultimate purpose. I knew with just a little planning and organization, my life could be easier and more fun. Putting things in order could really be a help in practical, everyday living.

Today, people comment about how organized I am, but really I'm just keeping up with things because I want my life to be easier. I want to enjoy all areas of life, and clutter and mess keeps me from those goals.

Many women truly struggle to become organized. The hard question for women today is "How can I possibly do it all?" Many women work part or full time in addition to raising children and trying to keep a home. As if this weren't challenging enough, today's American woman typically experiences more isolation than women in the past. Grandparents and the extended family usually live far away and are unable to help. Although we have superb labor saving devices today, the labor those devices saved was everyone else's, not the mother's. In earlier centuries, all the domestic chores were done in social groups. I'm not advocating that we return to beating our clothes clean at the river and churning our own butter, but at least whether she birthed it or hired it, a wife used to have help. Now, instead, a woman is surrounded by powerful technology (not necessarily a bad thing) but too often this superwoman finds herself standing alone.

If you are beginning to feel like I felt when the rain was coming down on me, just remember that you are *not* alone. Everyone has to plan, sort out, prioritize, and schedule some aspect of their life. This can be difficult for some people. And because organizing is difficult, other areas of their lives may stay difficult, too. If you are a woman who wants to accomplish the best you can in life but are having a hard time, you are the one I wrote this for. The goal of this book is to make organizing simple, and more importantly, a way of life.

Why should we need to be organized? Being organized will give you more time for the most important people in your life, your family. But beyond that, the Bible shows that God is a God of order (Gen. 1:1–31). Order creates peace, calmness and efficiency. God created one thing at a time, each on a specific day. He organized his creations until he was ready to create the best: us.

However, our modern lifestyle attacks this example of godly order. A spirit of self-centered independence dominates our culture, making rebellion against any authority figure, including God, fashionable. This is a complex issue, but one result of the modern "me first" spirit has been fractured homes. Women used to learn the secrets of running the manor from extended family. If you've had that privilege, you are unusual. The home seems to be the place that receives the least attention in today's fast-paced lifestyle.

With more than 80 percent of women age twenty-five to fifty-four working by the year 2000, we can certainly wonder if anyone will be home to take care of it. In Titus 2:5, the women of Crete (where Titus pastored) were encouraged "to be sensible, pure, workers at home." However, with the majority of women working outside the home, it will take extraordinary organizational skills to keep their homes in working order. Many of these women would prefer to stay at home and not work. Women who must work are sometimes overcome with guilt, believing they are abandoning their families and their duties at home. But even a working woman's family can feel cared for if that woman creatively manages her time.

Scripture shows us women who worked. Lydia, a single, working woman, was a dealer in expensive fabrics (Acts 16:14–15). Priscilla, also, was a working wife who made tents with her husband (Acts 18:2–3). You'll find another model of a godly working woman in the book of Judges, where Deborah led Israel. The paramount quality of all these women is that they were spiritual women who followed God's will for their life, whether in or out of the home.

This concept is the main point in organizing your life. Whatever you are called to do, first make sure it lines up with what God would have you do; and second, make sure your attitude lines up as well. Being a stay-at-home mom doesn't automatically ensure an efficiently run household. Every wife and mother must give her very best in order to excel in all her responsibilities.

In biblical days, the Jewish laws were clear: The woman's priority was in the home. She was to take care of all the household needs, her children, her husband, strangers, the poor and needy, and guests. The wife who faithfully held to these responsibilities was held in high regard by her family, in her synagogue, and in the community.

Likewise, women today, whether at work inside or outside the home, should still be accountable to take care of their homes and families. To do that, they must be organized.

As I was working on this chapter, the phone rang. It was my younger sister calling. She has two little girls, ages one and four. In addition to caring for them and her husband, she works outside her home three or four days a week. I knew her life had been hectic after her second daughter had been born, and as we talked she confessed her frustration. "You know, Lane, this has been the hardest year of my life. Now that the baby's a year old, I'm finally starting to catch up a bit. But it's so hard to get everything done. I have to think, to plan all the time. It isn't easy." I realized afresh the reason I wanted to write this book. I wanted to give some good, sound advice to women who want to get their lives in better balance.

That balance may begin with realizing, no, it isn't easy. Once we realize it isn't easy, and stop expecting it to be, we can change some of our attitudes and our methods of doing things. Change may produce discomfort, but if you keep doing things the same way when that way isn't working, you produce greater discomfort. Just a few changes here and there can make a tremendous difference in the way your life works. I know that we each can do it. We just have to redirect our thinking.

Don't settle for mediocrity. We are to work "heartily" for the Lord (Col 3:23). You are responsible for what God calls you to do for your family. His plan for others may be different than his plan for you or me, so ask yourself if you are glorifying the Lord with the way you are running your life now. Only you know the true answer.

Perhaps you don't know how to answer. If you're not quite sure how you're supposed to run a household on the Lord's behalf, God has already given us a wonderful example in Proverbs 31. Traditionally, the poem that begins at verse 10 was recited by husbands and children at the Sabbath table on Friday night. It portrays a wise, idealized wife, and indicates how God wants us to organize our lives his way. By following this scriptural example, our lives will take on a whole new dimension: lives of order, lives of love, and lives of balance.

My prayer for you, reader, is that the information and tips I give in this book will encourage you and help motivate you to be more of the godly woman God has called you to be, able to accomplish more than you ever thought possible. The Proverbs 31 woman has a lot to teach us, because "she opens her mouth in wisdom, and the teaching of kindness is on her tongue" (verse 26). This book will help you hear her.

BE AN
EXCELLENT WIFE

An excellent wife, who can find?
For her worth is far above jewels.
—Proverbs 31:10

HAT A LOVELY comparison! I've always wanted to be an excellent wife. But this goal is harder to achieve than I realized. I remember waking up as a newlywed right after the honeymoon, the first morning in our new apartment, ready to be that excellent wife. Of course, moving boxes were everywhere, but since I am a drill-sergeant at heart, I knew I could get everything shipshape in no time. With my expert efficiency, I told my husband just what he needed to do to help me with the job at hand. Unfortunately, he did not appreciate my orders. He left in a huff for the park with his football. I was left to wonder what had gone wrong. After all, I just wanted to be an excellent wife.

Well, I believe that if you're reading this, you are also striving to be an excellent wife. And having this goal is the first step in becoming organized. It is the first step because when you begin to build a strong oneness with your husband, you'll have less stress overflowing from your marriage into the other areas of life. This creates an ascending spiral, because as you begin to organize those other areas of life, you'll begin to have more time for your husband and your family. With reduced stress, you'll have time to build a relationship based on mutual respect and love. You can be a great wife, even if you think you never could be. I believe God placed this "excellent wife" verse at the beginning of this passage to show the importance of building on your marriage. When you take this first step in getting organized, other areas of your life will become more focused and balanced.

To build your marriage, you need to set practical goals. That was my mistake on that beautiful Saturday morning after our honeymoon. I was trying to do everything in one morning. That wasn't practical. And I was trying to make decisions for two people, without asking my husband what he wanted to do. If I had asked, I would have discovered that on that beautiful, sunny day, a trip to the park together was more important to him than unpacking.

I had to learn to take one thing at a time. As you begin to organize your life, don't try to do everything at once. Set realistic goals and objectives. The best way to start is to choose what area you want organized first. It might be a special room in your home, or a way to organize more time for your family. But the area I believe is the foundation for all other areas is working on being an "excellent wife." The Proverbs 31 woman has a wonderful bond and trust with her husband, and because of this relationship, she is able to accomplish much.

It's important to learn to communicate with your husband. Be available to talk to him day or night. After talking together, you may want to write down what the two of you would like to accomplish in your family, relationships, finances, work, and, of course, home. By setting goals, you'll be striving toward something instead of heading toward everything at once and nothing in particular. Your husband can be your biggest supporter and helper as you begin to organize your home and your life.

For her worth is far above jewels.
—Proverbs 31:10

Please remember that your worth, who you are in the eyes of the Lord, is never measured by what you do. Your worth is based on the work Jesus Christ did on the cross. Your responsibility is accepting his work on the cross into your life personally, and then living your life the best you can, letting your life give glory to God. By following his Word and organizing your life around those words, you will be following the path he has for you.

Nevertheless, this verse is such a compliment. If a man can find "an excellent wife" then he has something very valuable. In fact, she is worth more than jewels! May we become more valuable than jewels to our husbands.

Her husband has full confidence in her
and lacks nothing of value.
She brings him good, not harm,
all the days of her life.
—Proverbs 31:11–12, NIV

Her husband trusts she will feed the children well, keep up their home, and be there for him in attitude and action. In fact the very center of his life—his heart—trusts in her. What a blessing to have someone trust you completely! She never speaks evil of him or defames his character to others. He sees his wife as trustworthy and so she has great influence with him.

Due to her trustworthiness and her careful stewardship, his life continues to get better. He is able to totally concentrate on his work for he knows he can leave her with the great responsibility of running the household and raising their children. When the Proverbs 31 woman says she will do something, she does it, because her husband's comfort, success, reputation and joy is her delight.

I know sometimes we don't feel this kind of devotion to our husbands. No one does 100 percent of the time. However, by focusing on putting your life in order and in line with what God wants you to do, you can grow your attitude toward a more positive feeling. By making your life more balanced, you'll be able to do more for others, especially your husband.

> *Her husband is known in the gates,*
> *When he sits among the elders of the land.*
> —Proverbs 31:23

One of the most important uses of the gates of an ancient city was for holding court. Stone seats were provided for the judges. These gates compare to our modern courthouse. The gates were also popular meeting places for the people. Since they were connected to the walls that surrounded the cities, the gates were the main way into and out of the city, making them very important—"the chief place of concourse" (Prov. 1:21 KJV). And the Proverbs woman's husband was well known there. He wasn't just sitting with the elders to waste time while she was doing all the work. He was sitting there as one of the most respected citizens of their town, helping to create law and order. Since the Proverbs 31 woman is capable, her husband is free to pursue his responsibilities for his work and for his community. She encourages and supports him and has confidence in his abilities. This positive attitude carries over to her husband having a good reputation in his town as a leader.

Proverbs suggests that when you give first to your husband, then to others, this giving will come back to you full circle in the form of homes and communities full of security and love. Being a devoted wife is one of the foundation stones for balance and order in all areas of your life.

How do you become this devoted, excellent wife? The following tips may help you apply Proverbs 31:10–12, 23 to your life. Some of these tips will be obvious to you, while some might strike you as too demanding. Don't be dismayed or guilt-ridden. My intent is for these tips to help motivate you to be the wife you know your special husband needs.

Keep a Right Attitude

Marriage is a partnership which requires teamwork, mutual respect, oneness, and intimacy. Your love for your husband should encourage you to act toward him unselfishly, looking out for his needs, giving of yourself. This does not mean that you are to be subservient to him, but to honor him as your husband who God has placed in your life to guide and love you. Many women are repelled when they hear "Wives, submit to your husbands" (Eph. 5:22 NIV). However, the verse preceding it shows the meaning of marriage the Apostle Paul was trying to convey: "and be subject to one another in the fear of Christ" (Eph. 5:21 NASB). Each person in a marriage is to give to the other in love and humility, respecting the position that God has required. The husband is the head of the wife (as a captain is the head of a ship) but he also is required to "[give] himself up for her" (Eph. 5:25 NIV); in other words, die for her. How sad for wives and families when both partners try to rule the other instead of submitting to each other.

When your husband asks you to do something for him, try to do it without complaining or forgetting. We truly do reap what we sow, and if we do for our husbands with a sweet spirit, I believe they will do everything they can to help us. Of course, there are husbands who are difficult to live with! In that case, pray, and ask God to honor your efforts. The way we act is so much more important to the health of our families and home life then we will ever know. In *The Living Bible*, 1 Peter 3:1 says, "Wives, fit in with your husbands' plans; for then if they refuse to listen when you talk to them about the Lord, they will be won by your respectful, pure behavior. Your godly lives will speak to them better than any words." Organize all aspects of your life so that you are there for your husband when he needs you.

Respect your husband's job and give him the time he needs to do it well. Try not to call him too often at work or complain when he has to travel. With some of the downsizing in today's work force, our husbands need all the support we can give them. Pray for him to be successful in his job and for God to bless his efforts.

Never lie or be deceitful to him.

Recognize that you cannot fulfill all his needs. Encourage his interests in things outside the family. This may be hard when there are small children at home, but at minimum, work out ways where he can pursue his interests as well as help you at home.

Never try to come between your husband and his family and friends. Try to be a friend to his mother and never put her down or criticize her around your husband.

Don't forget to laugh! Let your marriage and your home be full of laughter and joy.

Go the extra mile, as a wife, a friend, a child of God. We are here for a purpose. Let's give this stay on earth everything we've got.

Remember to pray for your husband every day. This is one of the most loving things you can do for him. If you need extra motivation, try reading 1 Corinthians 13 at least once a week.

Take Time to Listen

Try always to be there for your husband. Put him first in your life. Care about his needs and listen to him. Be involved in his life. Adapt to his life. Remember, Eve was created to be Adam's helper. "Then the LORD God said, 'It is not good for the man to be alone. I will make him a helper suitable for him'" (Gen. 2:18 NIV).

Show a genuine interest in his work and in his hobbies.

Be respectful of his friends and be interested in them.

Occasionally, ask your husband his preferences. I have even asked mine what he likes and dislikes the most about me. (Note for the faint-hearted: don't tackle that issue unless you're braced for an honest answer.) I really do want to know what my husband thinks and feels so I can work on any area that might cause a division in our relationship. His preferences will surface one way or another, anyway; often the easiest way to learn them is in mature conversation.

Be an Encourager

Do everything you can to build up your husband's confidence. Try not to ever belittle or criticize him. Don't be the enemy. Remember you married because you wanted to be together. Keep that thought with you always.

View your husband as a gift from God. (And it isn't returnable!)

Express appreciation to your husband freely. Let him know how much you appreciate all he does. Don't hold back the compliments.

Focus on His Good Points

Whenever you find yourself being critical of your husband, think back on how you fell in love with him in the first place. Rekindle those feelings and attitudes. Begin to love him again, to listen and be friends again.

Be tolerant of his bad habits. Does he keep making a mess in the kitchen? Try to remember when he took all the kids away for an afternoon so you could have some free time.

Praise your husband in front of your children. Remind them that he is the head of the family and that all major decisions must first be approved by him. This will help teach your children respect and honor for their future spouses.

Do Practical Things for Your Husband

Try to keep your focus on your main job, which is to be a wife. Sometimes, when I am working hard on a project I put all my best energies and thoughts on the project and save little for my husband. He should be top priority.

Find out what your husband would like for dinner, and try to cook those things.

Keep your checkbook balanced and don't spend over your means or your budget. He needs to be able to trust you with the family finances.

Keep yourself in good shape. I know this is difficult after the birth of a child, but try to keep your body fit, your hair clean, your clothes pressed and your general appearance healthy. It honors our husbands when we try to look nice for them.

When your husband comes home from work each evening, get up and meet him. You need to honor your husband at all times, and this shows him that he is very special to you.

When your husband first arrives home after work, try not to bother him with problems right away. You'll be able to sense when he has "decompressed" a bit from a stressful day. Then when you do share problems, he will be more rested and ready to hear.

Be on time. No one likes to be kept waiting. Begin to organize yourself so you can be on time.

Let Your Husband Be Your Best Friend

Share your life with him first. Even though we have special girl friends, our husband should be our first and best friend.

Be ready and willing to share emotional, physical and spiritual intimacy with him.

Play with your husband. Try to find activities you both like to do—then do them. My husband and I love to take walks after dinner. It seems to be the best time to talk and be alone together. We also play sports together and swap books with each other.

If you are unable to act on any of the tips above because of a break in your relationship with your husband, ask God to love him through you. Sometimes, only God can bridge the gap between you. You might want to go to a Christian counselor who can teach you and your husband time-tested tools in conflict mediation. If you follow these steps and especially if you honor your husband, God can restore your relationship. Marriages need to be led by God and centered on him to succeed.

Back in 1931 Eleanor Roosevelt wrote an article called "Ten Rules for Success in Marriage" (reproduced on the next page). Though the language is dated, I was surprised to see how little has changed. I believe the advice is as relevant today as it was then!

Proverbs 31:10 sets the tone for all the rest of that chapter of Proverbs. How you see yourself as a wife will influence how you see yourself as a mother and a house manager. An excellent wife finds that the reduced stress gives her a boost toward organizing the rest of her home and life.

Love is patient, love is kind, and is not jealous; love does not brag and is not arrogant, does not act unbecomingly; it does not seek its own, is not provoked, does not take into account a wrong suffered . . . bears all things, believes all things, hopes all things, endures all things. Love never fails.

—1 Corinthians 13:4–8

Ten Rules for Success in Marriage

1. Have a plan, some central idea, as definite a pattern for your life as possible and a clearly understood object for the joint project.
2. Remember that sooner or later money is apt to be a cause of friction.
3. Apportion your time and energy, allowing each to share joint homemaking duties, as well as individual responsibilities.
4. Let neither husband nor wife strive to be the dominating person in the household.
5. Expect to disagree. Two people may hold entirely different views on many subjects and yet respect and care for each other.
6. Be honest.
7. Be loyal. Keep your differences to yourselves. The less said about your married troubles, except between yourselves, the better. The feeling that many young married people have—that they can complain to their parents when things do not go just right—is bad for them and brings more serious trouble later on.
8. Talk things over. When hurt, do not keep it to yourself, brooding over it. Meet every situation in the open. Troubles that seem momentous quickly vanish when frankly dealt with.
9. Avoid trivial criticisms. Grumbling and complaints use up the vital forces of man or woman.
10. Keep alive the spirit of courtship, that thoughtfulness which existed before marriage. Look for traits in the other that can be admired and praised. You can accomplish much by stimulating self-confidence in your partner.

As for the in-laws, offer as little advice to the newly married couple as possible, preferably none.

—Eleanor Roosevelt, 1931

Bringing Home Chapter 1

An excellent wife, who can find?
For her worth is far above jewels.
The heart of her husband trusts in her,
And he will have no lack of gain.
She does him good and not evil
All the days of her life.
Her husband is known in the gates,
When he sits among the elders of the land.
—Proverbs 31:10–12, 23

This chapter explains that the basis and foundation for being an organized woman begins with working on your relationship with your husband. Since the Proverbs woman was called an excellent wife, she can be an example for us.

DISCUSSION QUESTIONS

1. How would you describe "an excellent wife"?
2. What can you do to encourage your husband's trust?
3. What are some things you can do to show your husband good and not evil?
4. How can you build our husband's reputation *in* the family (especially with your children) and *outside* the family?
5. What tips from your own experience that strengthen your marriage could you add to this chapter?

PERSONAL APPLICATION:

- Ask yourself, "Do I need to change my attitude toward my husband?" If so, ask God to help you.
- What could you do this week which would help you become a more "excellent wife?"

2
PLAN YOUR SHOPPING,
COOKING, & TRAVELING

She is like merchant ships;
She brings her food from afar.
—Proverbs 31:14

OU MIGHT REMEMBER pictures of old sailing ships from your history books. Ships were the primary means of transporting goods between countries. However, sailing them was dangerous because of many problems including unexpected storms. Comparing the Proverbs 31 woman to one of these ships is a high compliment because it reveals she will do almost anything and go almost anywhere to obtain food for her family.

Doing so requires a great deal of effort and energy. I grew up in a family of seven children, and many of my childhood memories were of my mom in the kitchen cooking. She made us birthday dinners (anything we requested!) and birthday cakes. In the South where we lived it was the custom to cook big meals every night. It wasn't until I was a mother that I fully realized how hard that was. Unfortunately, most people don't cook real meals for their families anymore. And sometimes just dialing the delivery pizza number seems like a hardship! Perhaps we need to reevaluate our job description as the cook for the family. How can we show our families we love them by our cooking? And what meals could we cook that won't take all day but will be tasty and nutritious?

Food is such an important part of our lives. From the moment a baby cries out her first breath, she is ready to nurse. Food becomes not only a way to keep our bodies alive, but also a source of comfort and love. Every holiday and special occasion is usually centered around food. Food is used to feed our bodies, but food also has a deep and lasting emotional purpose in our lives.

Because of this, the buying and cooking of food is important to the emotional well-being of your family. For some women, cooking is an easy part of their lives. They do it naturally. But for myself and many other women, cooking and the time involved can be a large obstacle in the smooth running of their household. Even though I can keep up with most everything in my life, cooking the evening meal can push me right over the edge. So I really have to work at organizing my meal planning and shopping to have enough time to cook a decent meal for my family. Even though I am naturally an organized person, still I don't want to cook.

So, I have to work at it. I have to put myself aside and do for my family first. Maybe selfishness is the root obstacle to being an organized woman.

Whatever the reason, here are some helpful tips as you shop for food, cook, and organize your kitchen. In this second step towards becoming a more organized woman, we get down to the basics of running a household and taking care of the family. Begin to look at the planning, shopping, and cooking in simple ways instead of as monsters that can consume you. Begin by writing down the best foods you could prepare for your family and go from there. Remember, cooking is a tangible way of showing your family that you love them.

Plan Meals Ahead

For each night of the week, predetermine a set item or theme. Here's how I do it:

Mondays My husband travels some during the week, but is usually home on Monday nights. So I like to prepare one of his favorite meals, a basic meat and vegetable dinner.

Tuesdays Our girls attend AWANA at our church on Tuesday nights and have to leave early. That night I prepare a quick pasta dish they like.

Wednesdays I like to use any leftover meat from Monday night, such as a ham or roast. I add fresh vegetables to it for our meal.

Thursdays We usually eat Italian type meals on this night because my family loves spaghetti, lasagna, etc. (You could have different themes such as Mexican or Chinese, or even rotate several themes.)

Fridays We indulge on Fridays and let the girls order pizza. This is usually our family night, and ordering pizza has become a special tradition for our family.

Saturdays I don't plan a particular meal for this night unless we are having company. Usually, my husband and I have a date night. If the weather's nice, we might cook out. Keeping this night flexible helps me in my planning.

Sundays Since our first year of marriage, when I was working and going to school, we have gone out for lunch after church on Sunday. My husband grew up having a large Sunday meal at his grandmother's each week and he wanted to continue this tradition. Because we eat a large meal at noon, Sunday night is usually a light meal such as grilled cheese sandwiches and tomato soup, pasta, or leftovers. This is the meal the whole family helps with, the time when our girls learn to cook.

As you can see, having a pre-set dinner theme helps me in deciding what I have to cook each night. It also helps me in grocery shopping.

Shop Efficiently

Shopping can become addictive and a tremendous time waster. Designate one day a week for shopping. This day could also be used for other shopping errands. I like to grocery shop, go to the post office, bank, dry cleaners, and a general store like Target in one day. If that is too much shopping for one day for you, have a day designated for grocery shopping and another for clothes, presents, errands, etc. Make good lists of everything you need to do, keeping in mind where the stores are located in your town. You will save gas and time. By keeping your shopping on particular days, your week will be freed up for doing things you want to do. Jumping in the car for little things ends up taking big chunks of time out of your life.

Use coupons. If your grocery store markets double-coupons, you could easily save eight to fifteen dollars a week. This is a great way to be a good steward, as well as helping your husband with finances.

- Cut coupons and make your grocery list at the same time. I like to grocery shop on Mondays. On Sunday night, I sit down with the coupon sections from the paper and cut out new coupons. I then go through my other coupons and set aside the ones I will use at the store the next day. Then I make my grocery list, incorporating the coupons with it.

- Years ago, I separated and stored my coupons by category. Never again! Trying to keep up with all the coupons took too much time. I now keep my coupons in one envelope with a rubber band around them. I can look through the whole stack in a few minutes, pull out the ones I want to use and I'm ready to go. (If you're Internet-savvy, check **www.valupage.com** for coupons.)

When preparing your grocery list, check your master calendar and decide which nights you need to cook. List the meal you want to prepare for each night and pull those recipes. (This would be a good time to add those recipes that are special to your family on the days that work the best.) Then make your grocery list from these recipes.

- Sort through your recipes and pull out your favorite ten or fifteen to use on a regular basis. Pull out recipes that are *yours,* that is, those you enjoy making and ones people identify with you. This tip has really helped me. I had been trying to cook everything I saw in the food section of the newspaper and my cookbooks! Don't get bogged down with a lot of cookbooks unless it's your hobby. Stack these favorite recipes near your shopping list and it will make your weekly planning much easier.

- Make your grocery list to follow the layout of your grocery store. You will finish your grocery shopping faster, without backtracking.

- Buy according to the sales. Read the store ads in your newspaper and plan your menus accordingly. For example, if boneless chicken breasts are on sale, use recipes that need chicken breasts. You can save up to 40 percent simply by shopping sale items.

Keep a grocery list on the refrigerator door. Show it to family members and tell them to write down items that are needed. This is especially helpful when your children become teenagers. Many times my daughter will cook or make a snack, using items without my knowledge. If she writes these on the grocery list, I know to buy them. Encourage family members to list anything else they need as well, such as school supplies or presents for a birthday party. Keeping this list has been a real time saver for me.

As soon as you open a new container of something, such as peanut butter or margarine, add it to your grocery list. That way, it will be bought and stored in the pantry or refrigerator when it's needed. Nothing is as frustrating as needing mayonnaise for a turkey sandwich, only to realize that the jar is empty and there's none in the pantry! So, buy and store away. More importantly, though, needing items you don't have forces those time-wasting extra trips to the store. The list forewarns you so you can stay organized.

Keep emergency products on hand. This would be such items as powdered milk for snow days, bread in the freezer, and flashlights in the kitchen and each bedroom. The Proverbs 31 woman looked "well to the ways of her household" (v. 27) and we should too.

When you have very young children, grocery shop at night after they are in bed and your husband is there to watch them. This way you can shop without crying children. It will also free up your day so you can spend more quality time with them at home or at the park (unless, of course, the shopping trip is your outing together for that day). Usually, though, I preferred shopping without the children because I could shop faster and was able to concentrate better.

Shop for special holiday dinners or for company the day before you have to cook. That way you avoid shopping, cooking and cleaning all in one day and won't be exhausted.

Plan Your Cooking

The important thing about cooking is that you are building relationships in addition to fueling bodies. Control your cooking, instead of letting cooking control you.

Cook simply. Instead of using ten ingredients and one hour making a side salad, cut up fresh fruit or have a simple tossed salad. Instead of making a complex casserole, broil fish or meat in the oven and add fresh, sautéed vegetables. If you don't want to spend a lot of time cooking, you really don't have to.

Every morning, know what you will be cooking for dinner that night. Nothing is worse than five o'clock approaching without having a clue what you will cook. If the meal is planned, you can pick up missing ingredients when you are out during the day.

Try designating one day a week to cook. I like to cook on Mondays. Later in the week, I use some of what I cooked or froze. Consider cooking one large piece of meat such as a ham, roast, or turkey breast and then using it with different vegetables for different meals during your week. That way you are not starting from scratch each night.

Designate one day a month as a baking day. Bake breads, muffins, and cookies to freeze. I have a poppyseed bread recipe which people seem to love that freezes well, so I set aside a whole day each month to bake poppyseed bread. I can usually make twenty-one loaves at one time. I wrap each one with aluminum foil, place it in a freezer bag, and label it. Then I'm ready for Christmas gifts, house guests, or a special treat for my family.

Consider cooking with a friend. Buy your food in quantities and cook two or three freeze-proof recipes together. Double or triple recipes and freeze. Then these meals are ready whenever you have a busy day, or if you need to give a meal to someone else. We are not always free to cook for that sick friend or new neighbor, so having a dish already in the freezer helps. I have a casserole recipe and breakfast bread I bake in batches, then label and freeze. It is also nice to have a meal in the freezer when you return from a trip.

Use Ziploc freezer bags to freeze foods. That way the baking dishes you prefer to use aren't in the freezer for a long time. Disposable aluminum pans work well also. Use square or rectangle shapes instead of round ones. They are easier to stack in your freezer and save space.

Use a crockpot. This can free up your time when you are gone all day and want dinner ready when you come home. Put recipe ingredients in the crockpot in the morning and you will have a wonderful dinner that night.

Use cooking bags. I have really enjoyed using these the last few years. I even use them to cook my Thanksgiving turkey. You can put meat and vegetables in the bag and the cooking time is much shorter than regular cooking. The best part is, when you are ready to clean up, just throw the bag away and the pan is clean. Use a cooking bag when taking a dish to a sick friend. No dishes to return, and the turkey breast or roasted chicken is a nice alternative to the basic lasagna casserole.

Become friends with your butcher. His advice on how to cook different kinds of meat and fish can be helpful. You can also ask him to cut steak into strips or cubes for Stroganoff or shish kebobs.

Enlist family help. They can help in the decision-making process of "What's for dinner?" and they can help cook. As your children get older, have them help you with the meals. Even small children can help with simple tasks. The best time to have them begin cooking is a weekend meal when you are not in such a hurry. My children started to cook on Sunday nights. My husband supervises and I get a break. Don't hesitate to delegate. You can't do it all.

Organize Your Kitchen

Go through your kitchen with the eyes of a time manager. Rearrange items for better efficiency. Where do you make sack lunches? Put bread knives and baggies close by, along with a cutting board if you have one. Where do you do most of your cutting? Have your sharp knives nearby. Dishes and glasses need to be next to the dishwasher, and pots and pans near the stove. Some of these suggestions are obvious, but sometimes we do things by habit. Take a new look at your kitchen and organize it to be a better work area.

Go through your cabinets and clear out everything you don't use, especially those empty butter containers. Streamline every drawer and cabinet. Use silverware holders, shelves, hooks, etc.

Clean out everything under your sink, leaving just what you need on a daily basis. Keep a fresh sponge and counter cleaner handy and wipe counters down after every meal. Your kitchen will look and smell clean all the time with this one simple task.

If you need extra storage in your kitchen, look for stacking units that come on casters. You can roll them wherever they are needed. Look for other items to help organize your kitchen. Browse through kitchen stores. They're full of organizing helps. Since the kitchen is the hardest area to run efficiently, this might be the best place to start your home organizing effort.

Delegate kitchen chores to your family. They can all help clean the kitchen and put their dishes in the dishwasher.

When your oven starts to look bad, clean it as soon as you can. The longer you wait, the harder the job gets.

Unload your dishwasher at night before you go to bed. As you unload, set out breakfast dishes. This way you'll be ahead in the morning and you can load the dishwasher before you head out for your day. If I didn't do this, my breakfast dishes might stay in the sink all day long.

Keep liquid soap by your sink at all times so you will be able to wash your hands and your children's easily and consistently. Use paper towels instead of cloth towels when their hands are very dirty, such as after school.

Plan Your Traveling

Just as the Proverbs 31 woman planned efficiently to feed her family well, so she had to travel to be able to help her family (v. 14). In those days, she probably didn't travel far. Still, just traveling to a neighboring town or to ports to see what the ships had brought involved preparations. She would have to load donkeys or camels with food, bedding and supplies.

We all remember the trip Mary and Joseph took to Bethlehem from Nazareth. It was only eighty miles or so. Our modern cars could drive that distance in an hour and a half, but in Mary's day, that journey took many days. The women of Israel had to be organized and able to prepare for long journeys.

In our day, people travel all the time. It has become a way of life. From commuters who drive an hour each way to and from work, to the men and women who travel to different states and countries for their jobs, people are traveling. And because so many women are working now, the need to be ready to travel at a moment's notice is important. Families are traveling as never before. Our family plans a spring break trip as well as a summer vacation each year, and the girls like to go to summer camp. Needless to say, all this traveling takes a great deal of planning and organizing. Here are some tips to help you organize your next trip better.

Pack and Plan Efficiently

Once you know a trip is coming up, start putting aside in one place items you know you will want to take. You'll have that much less to think about the day of packing.

If you know you will be taking a trip to a tropical destination during the winter, pack for it when putting away your summer clothes. Pack bathing suits, sundresses, and even your suntan lotion. Then when it is time to pack, you will already have most of the necessary items, including the clothes that were your favorites the previous summer.

When you begin to pack, lay out everything on your bed or on the floor first so you can see if you have enough or too much. Lay out everything that goes with each outfit: belts, hose, shoes, and jewelry. Count each day you will be gone and add or subtract outfits.

- Always take extra underwear and socks.

- Take your bathing suit. You never know if there will be a swimming pool, hot tub or a sun deck you could use.

- Keep a cosmetic bag ready at all times containing extras of items you use. Then all you have to add is the makeup you use every day.

- For short trips, wear the jewelry you want so you won't have to worry about packing or losing it.

If possible, clean your house and wash clothes before you leave. Your house will smell better, you will enjoy coming home more, and you won't have a double chore of washing your travel clothes along with those that were in the laundry room.

Put a loaf of bread and some milk in the freezer. You won't have to stop by the store on the way home. Since the milk takes a long time to thaw, take it out as soon as you get home.

Take Extra Steps to Ease Air Travel

Jet lag is a reality. Travel can wreak havoc on your sleep, especially when you cross several time zones. If possible, put your body on vacation two to three days before you leave home. Gradually move the times you eat and sleep so they coincide with the time zone of your destination. Do the same thing on your way home. A well-hydrated body adjusts to time changes faster, so if you drink plenty of nonalcoholic beverages during your flight, you'll transition out of jet lag more rapidly. When you reach your destination, immediately abide by your hosts' clocks. Eat when the locals eat, sleep when they sleep, and wake up when they do. The morning light will help your body reset its clock to the local time.

When traveling with children, let them help pack their own carry-on bag. Sometimes the very thing they want is something we think is wrong. But if it isn't too big to carry and it makes them happy, take it. Do take their favorite stuffed animal or blanket. A trip is not the time to wean them from these comforting friends. Carry some books you could read to them as well as books they could read or look at themselves. Talk about the trip beforehand and let them know your expectations and the rules for the flight. Explain that they have to sit with their seat belt on and that there isn't a lot of room to move. Usually, children adapt well if they know what to expect. You might also have them carry their own water bottle and small snacks.

When traveling by plane, try to take as few bags as possible. A carry-on suitcase is best so you won't have to go through baggage. If checking your bags, keep track of how many pieces you are checking plus what you are carrying on. This might sound elementary, but on one trip my family took, we checked twelve bags and carried on nine!

When arriving for a flight, drop your luggage off first at the curb-side check-in for your airline. Your luggage will have more time to make the flight and you won't have to lug it from the car.

More quick tips on handling possessions while en route:

- Tie a red scarf or ribbon on your bags to spot them easily.

- Carry important papers, eye glasses, toothbrush, contact lens solutions, hairbrush, prescription drugs, and other important items in case your bags are lost.

- Keep your airline ticket, passport, money and keys in the same place each time you travel. So many times in the past I've panicked, thinking I had lost my ticket, only to find it somewhere else. I have learned to take the same carry-on bag with me and to keep these items in the same place every time. If you combine your pocketbook and carry-on in one bag, you'll be less likely to lose it, and you'll have more room around your seat.

If you must leave your car at the airport, write down where it is. As silly as this sounds, you can forget. We have been gone four to five weeks at a time, and I can't always remember that far back.

When going through airline security, keep your eyes on all your items, especially the ones you hand the security guard. Immediately pick up your items before someone else can and retrieve the ones from the guard. I lost my camera by handing it to the guard and forgetting to ask for it back.

Keep plenty of reading material with you. Airline travel is different than car travel. You can't carry as much, yet you could very easily be caught waiting for hours for a delayed flight.

Look for the baggage bin number for your plane's luggage as soon as you get off the plane, and you'll find your baggage quicker. In most airports it's posted on the ramp leading from the plane to the terminal.

If renting a car, have one member of your traveling party stand in line for baggage and another for the rental car.

Make Car Travel Easy

Traveling with children in a car also takes preparation but at least they have more room. You can stop the car whenever you want and let them stretch their legs, which should be done about every two hours. They should still pack their own car-bag with their special toys and you should have your own supply of games to help prevent boredom. Some families place a small television between the front two seats so children can watch their favorite videos.

Car Emergency Kit

✓ Basic first-aid pack
✓ Basic set of tools
✓ Flashlight(s)
✓ Set of battery jumper cables
✓ Small throw rug (for kneeling on the ground for repairs)
✓ Work gloves and snow gloves if it is winter
✓ Blankets (if you get stranded at night)
✓ Bag of cat box filler or rock salt (for icy or snowy roads)
✓ Old scarf and man's belt (for emergency hose repairs)
✓ Old shower curtain (to cover the ground if you have to crawl under the car.)
✓ Some type of drink and food in the car, such as water and granola or energy bars.

When you travel in a car with young children, always have something for them to drink, eat, or hold such as a book, toy or stuffed animal. For babies and toddlers, be sure to have extra diapers and wipes. You could get caught in a traffic jam and not be able to get what your child needs for hours. Be prepared.

Fill your car with gas when you still have a quarter of a tank left. On trips, you never know how far it is to the next gas station.

Always have current maps and plenty of directions.

When leaving a restaurant or motel always make a quick table (or room) check. I can't tell you how many times my last-minute checks have saved items of mine I would've left behind.

Carry an emergency kit with you in the car (see sidebar).

If you're traveling in the U.S., you can find almost anything you might have left behind. Remember to relax and have fun!

The LORD your God . . . went ahead of you on your journey, in fire by night and in a cloud by day, to search out places for you to camp and to show you the way you should go.
—Deuteronomy 1:32–33

Bringing Home Chapter 2

She is like merchant ships;
She brings her food from afar.
—Proverbs 31:14

The basics of running a household are crucial in becoming an organized woman and taking care of the family. Tips on how to organize grocery shopping and cooking, as well as tips for traveling safely and efficiently, can come in handy.

DISCUSSION QUESTIONS

1. What is a good method you use in planning and shopping for food?
2. Share some of your money-saving tips for shopping.
3. Share some of your best and easiest recipes.
4. What is the hardest part about traveling? What could you do to make it easier?

PERSONAL APPLICATION

- What are some ways that you could help your family eat more healthily and economically?
- What can you do to make mealtime an exciting, anticipated event?

She rises also while it is still night
And gives food to her household
And portions to her maidens.
— Proverbs 31:15

THE PROVERBS WOMAN has taken a step toward managing her time. She has learned that the main reason to be organized is to have more time for the important things in her life, taking care of and spending time with her loved ones. As these verses show, she rises early to prepare food for her household. She would have to be a wise manager of her time and resources for this to occur.

All my close friends know that early morning is not my best time of the day. In fact, I will do almost anything I can to keep from waking up very early. I remember the best part of nursing a baby was not having to leave the bed to prepare food. Mom keeps on sleeping while baby does all the work.

So, as you can imagine, this passage of scripture is not my favorite. But I am thankful that God, in his great wisdom, placed it there, because it shows me what God thinks is important in the running and organizing of my household. And whether I like it or not, I need to be up in the morning to minister to my family.

I believe God does not want us sleeping in while our children get their own breakfasts and leave for school. Of course, there are always exceptions, such as an illness, but God shows us in this passage that running a household takes great sacrifice.

The people in biblical times kept one small lamp burning through the night. In fact, for a Palestinian peasant a lamp was considered the one expense that was a necessity. When the sun set, the door of the house was shut and the lamp was lit. Sleeping without a light was considered by most villagers to be a sign of extreme poverty. Since the lamp had a small amount of oil, someone had to wake up during the night and add more oil to keep the lamp burning. The wife assumed this responsibility so her family could sleep. Then, she would stay up and begin preparing for the day.

She also set the example for her servants. Since she worked so hard, they could do nothing less. She demonstrated leadership and set strong examples for her children. She believed she was "working as for the Lord" (Colossians 3:23 NIV).

The grinding of the grain was the most important activity of the day for women and was always the first thing done in the morning. Perhaps this is what the Proverbs 31 woman was doing in these verses.

One of the customs of that ancient time was to cease working and close up shops from noon to three each day. Probably, the women were getting enough rest during this time so they were able to "rise while it was still night."

In our time, the most sought-after but elusive goal is to have "time for everything." Ephesians 5:15–16 has been called the Bible's key to time management: "Therefore be careful how you walk, not as unwise men but as wise, making the most of your time, because the days are evil" (NIV).

To make the most of our time can also be translated as "making the most of every opportunity." It suggests an attitude toward living that sees every situation as the perfect occasion to do God's will and influence others for him. During these evil days, we are to live out the goodness God has placed in us through faith in Christ.

How much time do we have today? Time for prayer? Time to answer a child's question? Time to be interrupted by someone in need? Time to consider others during an inconvenience or delay? Time to call or write someone who needs to hear from you? May the Lord give us wisdom to grasp today's opportunities, "making the most of [our] time" for what's important to him and our families.

But to keep going from morning to evening caring for children and a household, you need more than just pure energy. A woman has to feel called and motivated by God to please both God and her family if she is to succeed. The following tips can help motivate you as you take another step toward becoming a more organized woman.

Set Goals

Plan your days, your weeks, your months and your year. Let every hour count for something so that at the end of the day you have accomplished something worthwhile. Don't let someone else set your goals. Think and pray about what goals you want for your life.

Establish goals. Studies show that the success rate for people who write down their goals is about ninety times greater than for those who don't. Take time right now to do this. Start with what you want to accomplish each day, each week, each month and for the current year. These goals could be in different categories:

- housework
- activities with your children
- activities with your husband
- personal goals for yourself

If writing down goals is difficult for you, begin with a daily to-do list. Write down each thing you need and want to do for tomorrow. List according to your priorities. Going to the grocery store might be more important than finding new wallpaper, so place it at the top of the list. Just checking off each item feels motivating.

Set annual goals for yourself—and your family. Every January, our family sits down and writes out our goals for that year in four categories: spiritual, intellectual, and physical for each individual, plus our family goals. I keep these goals posted by my desk. When I review them throughout the year, I'm encouraged to try to accomplish them.

Set five-year goals. This would be for larger projects: writing a book, saving up for a special vacation, getting your child ready for college. Many companies, at the end of each fiscal year, write goals they'd like to see their organization achieve over the next several years.

Set long-term family goals. Families can do the same thing to give their lives more direction. Asking your children where they see themselves in five years helps them to plan ahead and to realize that what they do today can affect their future.

Set Up a Command Post

Treat your homemaking job like any other professional occupation. You are the COO (Chief Operating Officer) of your household.

Make sure you have your own desk, even if it's just a card table.

- On your desk keep accessories just for you: transparent adhesive tape, scissors, ruler, note paper, your stationery.

- Have a special place on your desk for phone calls that you need to make. Keep pen and paper by all phones for taking messages. Making a list of calls to be made keeps me from feeling overwhelmed. I know if I can't get to these calls today, they'll still be there tomorrow, listed so I won't forget.

- Keep your telephone book up-to-date. When recording names, addresses and phone numbers, use a pencil, not a pen, so you can erase and revise when numbers change.

- Keep your desk as neat as you can. You won't lose important papers or phone numbers if your desk is organized. Purchase a file cabinet, folders, and hanging files if you have the funds and space to do so. Or, put folders in a small stand or box. Folders are excellent for organizing important papers, receipts, bills, and children's activities.

- If you use the same desk for your household bills as well as your home-based business, be careful to keep these separated.

Have a calendar close by, either near your phone or in your purse, and check it daily. I keep my calendar open on the middle of my desk to review often. All the family's activities are written on this calendar, as well as birthdays, anniversaries, and special notes.

- On Sunday night review the next week. Circle in red doctor appointments or anything else that must not be forgotten for that week.

- Check to see if there are birthdays or anniversaries listed on your calendar for the next week (or month, if that is easier). Add these names to your grocery list so you can pick up cards or presents.

- Every December, with red ink, fill in next year's calendar with important dates such as birthdays and anniversaries. This way, you will never forget someone special. To make sure you have the cards for those birthdays and special occasions, buy all the cards you'll need for the whole year and keep them in a certain place for use when needed.

Establish a Daily Routine

Have a five-minute quick-clean routine every morning (see Chapter 10). Keeping a house looking nice doesn't need to take hours and hours; five to thirty minutes can do wonders. I have a two-story house, so I straighten the downstairs at night before I go to bed, and the upstairs before I leave for the day. The goal is to keep your home picked up, clutter eliminated, and dirty clothes and trash in their correct places. If you have young children, plan which household task is important to do each day and have your children help with it. Make a game of it; they'll have fun and help you too.

Try to finish your tasks early in the day. This way you'll have more free time for your own projects and activities.

If you don't work outside the home full time, plan to be out of the house only every other day. You can stay caught up on laundry, phone calls, cooking, etc,. if you are home more.

Schedule a stay-at-home day every week. I chose Mondays because it helps me organize my week. This is when I do heavy cleaning and laundry, change beds, dust, and organize drawers or cabinets. I also cook a large meal for that night. If Monday doesn't work for you, find the day that's best for you and your family.

Schedule a "playing" day. I like Fridays. When the children were small, this is the day I would take them to the park, to the mall, or to a friend's house to play. Now that my children are older and in school, I use this day to shop or have lunch with a friend, play tennis, or just read. Even if I only have a few hours, I try to do something I really want to do.

Try to do laundry or projects before the weekend so you are free to be with your family. Saturdays should be for fun not work. Of course, large projects like finishing the basement or getting the yard ready for spring may have to be done on weekends. I just know our family feels closer if we do special things together instead of chores all the time. Those of you who work outside the home during the week will probably need to work on your chores on the weekend.

Schedule a set time when the whole family can work together on these. Then the rest of your weekend is free.

Set up traditions to help you schedule your week better. Our children like to have pizza every Friday night. I like it, too. It's one night I don't have to plan to cook. We also have traditions for holidays which I find helpful when it comes to planning.

Make the Most of Your Time

Scheduling our days and keeping up with our goals are difficult. The biggest problem for most of us is simply finding enough time. Here are some tips.

Reduce your choices and prioritize. In our busy lifestyles, there are too many choices to make, from which activity to be part of to which running shoes or fat-free salad dressing to buy. Sit down and determine the most important areas in your life. Then simplify and set priorities.

- Prioritize commitments. A good friend shared with me that at one time in her life she was involved in almost every club in her small town, besides helping at church and her children's school. After prioritizing, she decided to concentrate on just two areas of volunteering: her church and her children's school. In this way, she could give herself more fully to the Lord and to her family.

- Simplify your purchases. Buy just the amount of make-up or clothes or household items you really need. Yes, that Strawberry Liquid Face and Body Gel looks pretty, but do you really need this in your life? Maybe just a good, healthy soap can do the trick, reducing your costs and freeing space in your bathroom. I try to make buying choices based on what will keep my life as simple and as carefree as possible. "Stuff" brings more responsibility.

Get rid of everything you don't need. I have gone into every area of my house, throwing out what we no longer use and cleaning out the cabinets and drawers and closets. See Chapter 10 for details.

Learn to say no. For some of us, this is the hardest rule. We women are taught to do for others. I personally want to help everyone who calls me. But, if I say yes to everything, I am actually being selfish to my family. Since most activities people ask us to do are good things, it comes back to our personal goals and priorities. That is why it is vital to have these set for yourself. Then, if a request lines up with your goals and priorities, you can say yes. If it doesn't, you can say no and not feel you have let someone down. Being in balance and following God's will invites freedom.

Find your energy time and use this time for your hardest tasks and projects. When my children were little, my worst time of the day was when I put them down for their naps. I would just collapse, then feel guilty that I wasn't using this free time for chores. Finally I realized I'm a night person. Night is when I have the most energy. I began to nap when the children did. Then as soon as I put them to bed at night, I had several hours to work with no interruptions. I used this time to clean house, do laundry, iron, pay bills and sew. Of course, I was able to work at night because my husband traveled. When he was home, I adjusted to his schedule. If your husband doesn't travel or if you are a morning person, than obviously nights won't work for you. What is important is that you find your own energy time.

Don't be afraid to delegate. This is a hard area for me because I think I can do it all. I forget to ask for help. My husband reminded me that the less I do the more opportunities he has to help. This really opened my eyes. I realized I was doing a disservice to my whole family by not involving them in the running of the household.

- Assign chores to your children. Find a chart to hang in the kitchen and let your children choose the chores they want (make sure they are age appropriate). My children preferred me doing it all—at first. But now they have a sense of pride that they know how to clean and cook and will be able to take care of themselves one day when they are on their own.

- With your husband, write plans or lists of ways he could help you. Perhaps by sitting down with him and talking about your needs, he will be willing to help. Mothers of preschoolers especially need their husband's help.

- Find a friend, a neighbor or other family member that you can ask for help. This is especially important for single mothers.

- Review the chores you do that take too much of your time, and find a better way to do them. I've decided I don't have time to wash my car, so I pay the extra few dollars when I fill my car with gas and let the machine wash it.

- Hire a teenager. My husband doesn't like yard work, so we pay a teenager in our neighborhood to mow the grass. This frees Saturdays for family time and helps this young man earn some money. If you enjoy washing the car and mowing the lawn, look at other time-stealers in your routine and see if someone else can do them.

Time yourself. Set a time limit and race against the clock. Try to get your morning chores finished before lunchtime. If you accomplish that, reward yourself with a walk, a long phone call to a special friend, or a start on that extra project you have been wanting to do.

Don't let your tasks expand to fill the time. Set the time and shorten the time for the task. You will be the one in control of your day and the goals you want to accomplish. If you were working in an office and your boss said you could leave two hours early if all your work was done, most likely you'd work much faster than normal so you could leave. You can make this principle work at home, too. Recently, I set 9:00 PM as my goal to be finished with everything I need to do each night. This is a hard goal. I wander around listening to the news on television, making phone calls, and catching up on my laundry and before I realize it, it's late and I haven't sat down to read, which is what I've been waiting all day to do. So now I try to get the little things finished, the cats put away, and the lights turned out by 9:00 so I can go upstairs and have time just for me. I've even told my children that after 9:00, I will not help with homework or sign papers. This might seem harsh, but it makes them stay on task and become responsible for their own time management.

Stop procrastinating! Everyone, including myself, has times when they just can't do what they should do. For example, I knew I had a writing project to finish, but there was always something else crying for my attention. Finally, I stopped paying attention to those things and concentrated on what I knew had to be done.

- If what you are putting off seems an overwhelming task, break it up into manageable steps. Clean one room at a time instead of trying to do the whole house. Sometimes, the dread of a task is more stressful than the task itself. For example, we decided to finish our basement which meant we had to move everything stored there upstairs temporarily. I didn't think we could do it. But my husband just started carrying items upstairs, and as we worked together, it wasn't nearly as bad as I had thought it would be.

- Just do it! Begin on what needs immediate attention. For example, if you know you have to write thank you notes, get the stationery out of the box and onto your desk.

Perhaps address the envelopes. Then, when you are at your desk waiting on hold, start writing those notes.

- Focus on what is important about whatever you are putting off. If, for example, you can't seem to get your thank you notes written, focus on who they are for: special people in your life. Wanting them to feel your appreciation should be enough motivation to get on with the task at hand. This is how I tackle my struggle with cooking. I would procrastinate cooking dinner if I could. But keeping my family happy and healthy is what I focus on, not how tired I am at cooking time.

- Plan a special reward for yourself when your task is finished. Think of something you really like to do. Promise yourself you can do it as soon as you finish your task.

- Tell yourself you can't do something else you want to do until you have started on this goal. If my goal for the day is to plan the holiday party for my daughter's school, I put off my walk or phone calls I want to make until I reach that goal. Sometimes you must discipline yourself to do what you should do rather than what you want to do.

"Therefore, since we are surrounded by such a great cloud of witnesses, let us throw off everything that hinders and the sin that so easily entangles, and let us run with perseverance the race marked out for us" (Heb. 12:1 NIV). We must live every area of our lives with discipline and with a purpose for the Lord.

Have a Place for Everything

This is important if we want to keep our homes streamlined and organized. Plan a place for the daily newspaper and put it there as soon as you're finished with it. Keep all your tools in their proper place and teach your children to respect your property by doing the same. If you have a question as to where something should be stored, place it where you think it will be used the most. Another great reason for having a place for everything is that you won't spend precious time searching for items you can't find. I hate to lose things, so I am very motivated in keeping everything in its place.

Put things away. You will save hours of cleaning time plus hours of searching time if everyone remembers to just put things away when they are finished with them.

Establish a set place for everything. Go through every area of your house and straighten and organize to decide this. Always put the same things in the same places:

- receipts in your wallet
- tickets to upcoming events in a special place on your desk
- mail in a pre-determined in-box
- magazines and catalogs where they won't clutter
- newspapers in a tidy stack

Be ready to throw things away! The average person handles about three hundred items of paper a day (bills, mail, magazines, etc.). If you can't think of a use for an item now, toss it out now.

Hold a family meeting. Let each one know where things now belong in the home. Ask for their help. No one can keep a home organized without each family member's help.

As you come across items you don't want, set them aside in one area of your basement or garage. We call this area our garage sale area. When it gets full, we have a garage sale! This is also a great time to give away outgrown toys or items to someone who can use them.

Handle Paper Only Once

I'm sure you have heard this before but it is worth repeating. Have a set routine each day for when you will read the paper and dispose of it and when you will get the mail and dispose of it. When sorting mail, separate into five stacks:

To do. This stack is where I put papers or mail that need a response. Some examples would be an invitation to a party that requires R.S.V.P., a letter I need to answer, or a thank you note I need to write immediately. I have a special place on my desk for this stack. Some of you might prefer to use a basket to keep these in one place.

I also make stacks for my husband's and children's mail. I place my husband's mail on his desk and my children's mail at their place on the kitchen table. Then when they come home from school, they immediately see their mail when they get their snacks.

To pay. This stack is for all the bills. I also stack here anything from my children's school that needs a check, such as an upcoming field trip. I have one section on my desk for bills to be paid on the first, and another section for bills needing to be paid later in the month.

To file. Examples would be receipts, insurance forms, or decorating ideas from a magazine. If you are fortunate enough to have room for a file cabinet next to your desk at home, I suggest filing these immediately. However, most people prefer to place these in a bin or basket to be filed later.

To read. Isn't it great to have something to read when you're waiting in line or in a doctor's office? You might want to have a basket where you place articles, magazines, or books that you want to read. You can take this in the car with you and just grab what you want to read out of it.

I have a table next to my side of the sofa where I keep all my magazines. I try to keep this current. As soon as I finish a magazine, I give it away, throw it away or save it. (Since decorating is one of my passions, I just can't throw away my decorator's magazine for awhile!) I keep bookmarks in the magazines I'm reading so when I have a few minutes, I can pick up where I left off. When I see an article I like, I pull it out to make sure I won't forget to read it or file it.

To toss. Finally we come to the main stack: your wastebasket! Much of the papers and mail that we receive is junk. Don't let it clutter up your life. Make a quick decision on mail and throw away what you don't need.

Just remember, you save yourself hours every week by being organized with your mail and paperwork. You relieve yourself of undue stress when you look at the mail corner of your house and it is neat.

Put God First

This is one hint you probably haven't seen in many time management classes, but our Lord has to be first in every area of our lives for us to be successful. It is his will we are to follow every day. We must ask ourselves, "What am I doing with my life and with my time that will last forever?"

Becoming organized women should not be the main focus in our lives. We should want to be more organized so that we have more time to give to the Lord and his work. His Word and his people are the only things that will last.

Commit your works to the LORD,
And your plans will be established.
—Proverbs 16:3

Bringing Home Chapter 3

She rises also while it is still night
And gives food to her household
And portions to her maidens.
—Proverbs 31:15

Verse 15 reflects how the Proverbs 31 woman scheduled her days and nights so she was able to help others and was able to begin her day ready to go. There is value in scheduling your life so all areas will be well balanced.

DISCUSSION QUESTIONS

1. How do you begin each day? What time do you usually go to bed and get up in the morning?
2. How can you make the most of your time? Do you have time-stealers in your routine?
3. What would you include in your five-minute quick clean?
4. What traditions would you like to have scheduled in your life?
5. Do you find time every day for your most important priorities?
6. Do you have time every day with God?

PERSONAL APPLICATION

- Review how you spend your days, weeks, months and years. What could you change in your schedule so that you are making the most of your time and life?

4

BALANCE HOME
AND CAREER

She considers a field and buys it;
From her earnings she plants a vineyard.
She makes linen garments and sells them,
And supplies belts to the tradesmen.

—Proverbs 31:16, 24

NCE UPON A TIME, there was a young married couple who were blessed with the birth of their first child. Because they loved their child so much, they wished that the wife could stay home and raise the child. But the bills still needed to be paid. So the wife went out and found the ultimate perfect job. She could arrive at work by 10:00 A M, leave at 2:00 PM, and she was paid as though she were working full time! She could take their precious little baby with her to work so she could keep nursing and she could be home every day in time for his nap. While the baby napped, she was able to cook a delicious meal, wash and iron the clothes, clean the house and still have time to get herself beautiful before her husband came home. After playing with their child together, they would tuck him into bed and then have wonderful conversation over the excellent, candlelit dinner she had prepared in their clean and well-organized home.

So, how did you like this story? Well, "story" is the accurate word because it is a fairy tale. Real life does not look like this, as I think we would all agree. Wouldn't it be great if everything just clicked along as effortlessly as in the story? Wouldn't it be wonderful if women of today could keep their homes running perfectly, their children growing into hard-working young adults who never argued with their parents, their husbands happy and able to bring in an income with hardly any extra effort at all? I wish it could be like this, especially for single mothers, but the fact is we can't do it all or have it all.

I have to admit addressing the topic of women working is a challenge. Women are pulled in so many directions in today's world. The expectations placed on women today far exceed those from any other time in our history.

When my mother was raising her first three children, she didn't even have a car. Most families had just one car, and that was for the husband to use for work. She didn't have the health clubs, commitments, or weekly women's meetings that we women have in our life today. She took care of her family and home and she loved every minute of it, probably because she didn't have other things pulling her in different directions.

Today women are bombarded with opportunities and pressures to have a career, to "be somebody." But whenever the world tells me to do something, that is when I need to open God's Word and see what it has to say about the roles of women in the workplace and in the home. Titus 2:5 encourages women to "be sensible, pure, workers at home, kind, being subject to their own husbands, that the word of God may not be dishonored."

I believe this concept of loving and being devoted to our families as a way of honoring God is the principle that flows through Proverbs 31. As verses 16 and 24 point out, the Proverbs 31 woman worked. But how she worked, and why and when, are wonderful examples to us as we make choices in our life.

In today's world, balancing financial needs with a child's emotional well-being is complex and may require tough choices. I have no right to tell you whether you should stay home or leave home to work. That is a decision for you and your husband to make and a choice that can make a woman feel tremendously guilty. Each woman needs to ask the Lord what is best for her and her family. If you are a single mom, staying home with your children is not a likely option. You are likely the sole support of your family, and my heart aches for you.

But in homes where the husband is able to support the family and there are preschoolers, the wife should stay home and nurture the children. The family will reap tremendous benefits in later years because of this choice. I have a hard time when mothers who don't need to work but do so for extra material comforts. As unpopular as this perspective might be, I feel compelled to say mothers have to put their children's best interests before their own. If that means a career has to be put on hold or the old car needs to be driven another few years, so be it. Children are not acquisitions. They are precious human beings who need a parent guiding them every day. A day care center, used every day, will never offer them the care, instruction, security, and love that a parent can.

If you are struggling with this, sit down and review exactly how much money you bring home after deducting childcare expenses, new work clothes, dry cleaning, gas and parking, lunches and taxes. I have talked to many women who realized they were making only a small income after these were deducted. These moms have pointed out they would save money, with fewer doctor bills, if their pre-schoolers were home more. They would also spend less on take-out food and money spent to relieve stress.

If you are undecided about whether to work or not, read books on how it might impact your preschoolers. Burton L. White wrote a book entitled *The First Three Years of Life*. In it, he gives evidence that the first three years are vital to a child's development. He recommends waiting to go back to work until your child is at least three.

What can we learn from the Proverbs woman? She "considers a field and buys it; from her earnings she plants a vineyard" (31:16). This "excellent wife" is also an entrepreneur, a "working woman." She wants to increase the wealth of her family and is always on the lookout for things she can do. She first thinks through her purchases and then buys from her own earnings; her husband doesn't give her the money. She has learned how to save. But what type of "job" is this? She is working to help her family and the work is probably right in her own backyard. In other words, the field is probably next to her house, so she really has a "home-based" job!

She buys a vineyard because grapes and raisins are important products to a Hebrew family. During the months of September and October, the fresh ripe grapes are eaten along with bread as one of the principal foods. Then the grapes are dried in a corner of the vineyard, sprinkled with olive oil, and stored for winter use. Raisins were widely used as well. The Hebrew people would take the juice of grapes and boil it until it became as thick as molasses. This was called "dibs" and was eaten with bread or thinned with water for drinking. And, of course, the vineyard would supply the family with wine.

As you can see, the Proverbs woman made wise purchases for her family. Her goal wasn't to "find her identity" or to "get away." She used her God-given talents to bring in extra money and food to help her family. From helping and giving to her family, she found joy, contentment, and self-confidence.

> *She makes linen garments and sells them,*
> *And supplies belts to the tradesmen.*
> —Proverbs 31:24

And now we know the source of her earnings. She knew how to sew and she used this talent to bring in income for her family. What wisdom she possessed! Instead of spending her income on frivolous things, she spent it on things that would benefit her whole family.

Through the years, I have had many part-time jobs (part-time, because I simply could not leave my children in day care). I was fortunate that my husband could provide for our family, but we also were prudent in our spending. We didn't have furniture in the living room and dining room for eight years. I took full advantage of this, though, because I turned the dining room into a playroom. Since it was adjacent to the kitchen, I could keep an eye on my children all the time. After breakfast, they would play in their playroom until nap time or errand time. There was no television in the room, so they didn't ask to watch it. Only in the afternoons after their nap did they watch *Mr. Rogers' Neighborhood* or *Sesame Street* in the family room.

Even though people might have laughed at us because our home wasn't completely furnished, our children benefited. And that was what was important to me.

Our society today is very different from the time of the Proverbs women. According to *Time Magazine,* 68 percent of women with children under eighteen are in the work force compared to 28 percent in 1960. Fifty-three percent of women with infants now work. Women in Biblical times were considered disgraceful if they worked apart from their husbands in the marketplace or at a trade. They could only work at home making craft items, or in horticulture, selling the fruits of their labor.

When the Apostle Paul wrote his epistle to Titus, he gave some advice on how the believers should be living in their pagan society. He wanted them to present a clear testimony on how believers in Christ needed to live. In Titus 2:4–5, Paul instructs the older women in their actions to:

> encourage the young women to love their husbands, to love their children, to be sensible, pure, workers at home, kind, being subject to their own husbands, so that the word of God will not be dishonored.

The key here is that in whatever we do, the word of God is never to be dishonored. Someone has to take care of home, the children, and everything that revolves around the family, and God has primarily given women the responsibility. The value of this work, which was severely underestimated in the early eighties, is always there and constant. But working for our families and homes should be a joy. Today we have so many more conveniences in the home than in the time of the Proverbs woman. We don't have to grind our own grain, make our own fabric, or wash our clothes in a river. We now have more time to do more for our children, our neighbors, our communities. As Christian women, we need to remember that we are to pursue God's will. God makes it clear that we are to be responsible for everything that revolves around our home.

It would be wonderful if all women were able to stay home the majority of the time while raising their young children and, like the Proverbs woman, find jobs that could bring in an income from home. But I know that isn't reality for some women.

If you are a single mother, or a woman who must help your husband bring in enough money for the basics, it is not my intent to heap guilt upon you. You are the precious woman who has so little time to do it all; it is especially for you that I wrote this book. To keep up an outside job, the housekeeping responsibilities, and raise children, any woman has to be highly organized.

The following tips can help the working woman take another step toward being more organized.

Find the Right Job for You

Like the Proverbs woman, find a job that uses your talents, something you like to do. If you have very young children but you need to work, first look at options other than full-time work. Though you will not make as much money with part-time work as you would full time, the few years at home invested in your children will reap tremendous rewards.

Consider something you can do at home such as bookkeeping or secretarial services. Or sell goods or services from your home. Beauty companies such as Avon, Mary Kay, or Nu Skin are examples of home-based businesses that have made many women successful from their homes. If beauty's not your interest, there are a wide variety of other businesses to choose from: try nutritional food supplement companies such as ReLiv, or kitchen aids such as Pampered Chef or Tupperware. If you have an entrepreneurial spirit, start your own business. Women are earning money from home selling their own crafts or fashions, performing desktop publishing or graphic design, telemarketing, researching via the Internet, and more. A need for money does not automatically have to drive you out of your house. The rising use of the Internet and telecommuting by fax and e-mail make this the best era in decades for earning money from home.

Consider working in a hospital. I have friends who can work one or two twelve-hour nights a week while their small children sleep. The income from this is equivalent to working a full week. Some of you, like myself, might not be able to work all night without sleeping, but this is another option to consider.

Consider working at a church. Churches often have part-time positions available, either as a secretary or working in the nursery on Sunday mornings. Many churches hold a pre-school during the week. This is an excellent option for mothers of pre-schoolers. They can bring their children to the pre-school while Mom works.

Consider working at a school. Once children are in school, many women become teacher's aides or teachers themselves. They are home in the afternoons and on school breaks with their children. If you need to work and your children are in school, think about jobs that allow you to be home in the afternoons and during summer breaks.

If you are already working, look into a part-time position for the same company or ask about a job-sharing position. Many companies are eager to keep a good employee and will try to work out hours that work for you.

If your job requires traveling, look for ways to make the schedule work for your family. I speak at workshops, seminars and retreats. I try to schedule overnight retreats no more than once a month. Weekly seminars are scheduled so that I can be home in the afternoon. I also keep some days free for housecleaning and cooking. I always wish I could lead more seminars, but at this time in my life I can't. If your boss is requiring too much travel, talk to him or her about this. Your boss may not be aware of your particular situation.

Keep a Right Attitude

Be excited with the journey of life. It's easy to start thinking everything is too hard, that there's just too much to do. This is a mistake I make too often. If you feel life is too hard ask yourself, "What is missing? What is wrong?" Ask God to help you refocus on the life he has given you and to find the joy.

When you are at work don't feel guilty about not being home and when you are at home, don't feel guilty about not being at work. Leave office problems at the office so you will be available 100 percent to your family when you are home. Keep your life as balanced as you possibly can.

In your job, remember to please yourself too. Don't take on extra work just to please someone else. Set limits on how much you'll be available to others at work. Set a time when you know you need to be home with your family and stick to it.

Keep a daily to-do list and include at least one thing that you want to do, even if it's reading a magazine for five minutes. Have something on your list that will be enriching, restorative to your spirits, or simply fun. This is important to your emotional well-being.

Write a family mission statement. Ask your family what the most important thing to do together is. For one family, it might be eating dinner together every night. Another might want to have a family night once a week. This will help you to treat your family as more important than your business.

Be Realistic in Your Daily Goals

Remember, you can't do it all. Break the pattern of doing too much. Recognize your limitations. Try delegating more and asking for help, which is simply sensible management, not weakness. Think of yourself as the organizer of your day. Plan when you can do certain tasks so you won't be overwhelmed when it's time to go home.

Balance your tasks between priorities and demands. I define *priorities* as something important to you that you want to do, while *demands* are something important to someone else that you feel you should do. Doing only what you want is selfish, while doing only what others want is unendurable. Each day should contain both.

Make lists. Make grocery lists, Christmas present lists, things-to-do-today lists.

Put the urgent items at the top of the list. Then if you run out of time or energy, those tasks have been accomplished.

If you have a home-based job, keep it physically separate from the rest of the house. Work in a closed off area or room, with your own desk, phone, and other supplies. This will help you keep your home life and work life separate. Warning: if you run your home business from your bedroom, the visual reminder of the work piled up will prevent you from truly relaxing when you desire privacy or sleep. If possible, utilize a basement or spare room instead.

Maximize Your Time

If you work full time, hire outside help to keep up your house, and use more convenience foods or eat out. You need extra time for your family. You should not try to be a super woman and do everything. That leads to a stressed out mom that is no joy to be around.

If you are unable to afford hiring someone to help clean your house, schedule a day (or evening) every week when you can get the basics done, such as vacuuming and laundry. Then the rest of the week, you won't worry about how clean your home is and you can spend just a little bit of time keeping it up.

Use your lunch time for errands, exercising, or personal phone calls so you will have more time at home. (Remember to pack a lunch so you still eat something.)

Be smart when you use the telephone. Make notes about what you will need to discuss before you place a call. Keep the discussion brief and to the point. Always be polite and cordial, but stay on the subject. Try timing each call, ending the conversation when the set time is up. Leave detailed messages on answering machines so others can respond with an answer more quickly.

Avoid long lines, traffic, and other time wasters by living off-peak. Go to restaurants early, do your grocery shopping late at night or early in the morning, and buy Christmas gifts all year long.

When a holiday or special event is coming, do as much as you can early. I try to have everything finished for Christmas by December 1. This way I have time to enjoy the season and can go to parties and school and church functions for my children without the stress of trying to get ready for Christmas.

Be aware that saving money can cost time for yourself or your family. A buffet dinner for $4.99 sounds great, but if you have to stand in a long line and waste a lot of time, the $6.99 dinner across the street would really be cheaper. Your time is worth something.

Use every service you can afford to help you save time and energy. Two good examples: automatic deposit for your paycheck, automatic payment for your utility bills or mortgage.

Let your family know when they can and can't interrupt you. It is vital for all family members to understand the importance of your job and that distractions can hurt your productivity. This step will help you avoid getting caught in the crossfire of competing demands from your boss and your children.

Identify the hardest part of your day or the most stressful thing you do and change it if you can. When it is taken from your schedule or modified, you'll be able to do so much more. An example of this is trying to cook dinner on your busiest or longest day. It is hard to walk in the house at six and then try to put a meal on the table. Put something in the crockpot that morning before you leave for the day or let that be the night to eat out. Your day will go more smoothly if you take some stress out of it.

Remember, when you make a task easier, you don't just save time, you make your life better. "Does thou love life?" Benjamin Franklin once said. "Then do not squander time, for that's the stuff life is made of."

Realize if you work, you will have to be highly organized to get everything done at home. But also realize that you will have to be flexible. When things aren't going well, *you* are still okay! Our Lord can help us through anything we have to do and will give us the strength to accomplish everything we have to do.

"Come to me, all you who are weary and burdened, and I will give you rest."   —Matthew 11:28

Bringing Home Chapter 4

She considers a field and buys it;
From her earnings she plants a vineyard.
She makes linen garments and sells them,
And supplies belts to the tradesmen.
　　　　　　　　—Proverbs 31:16, 24

Today, more women are working outside the home. Balancing a career and home life is more of a challenge than ever. But the Proverbs 31 woman was able to do it all. We can learn from her example: what type of work she did, how she was able to do it, and who the work was for: her family.

DISCUSSION QUESTIONS

1. What are some ways you could bring in extra money without having to sacrifice time with your family?
2. Can you think of other tips for balancing a woman's home life and her work life?
3. What was the Proverbs woman's main motivation in working?
4. If you are exhausted from working full time, what could you change in your life to reduce your work load?
5. Remember that you can't do it all. Discuss the most important things you should do each day.

PERSONAL APPLICATION

- Take time to reflect on how your work schedule affects you and your family. Do you feel that any changes need to take place, or are you satisfied with how things are? Discuss with your husband any feelings you have, positive or negative, so that he can support and help you.

GET IN SHAPE

She girds herself with strength
And makes her arms strong.
She senses that her gain is good;
Her lamp does not go out at night.
—Proverbs 31:17–18

OR THE PROVERBS WOMAN to be able to accomplish everything in her day, she must have tremendous energy. She already is a strong woman internally because of her self-discipline, commitment to her family and love for her husband. But she also needs to work at having physical strength so she can be strong and healthy for them.

The household chores for the women in that day were very physical. Just to wash their clothes took tremendous time and energy. The women had to go to nearby sources of water—streams, pools, or watering troughs. There they would dip the clothes in and out, place them upon flat stones and beat them with a club. This type of work was hard but had to be done. The Proverbs woman had to keep herself strong to continue working at everything she had to do.

Fortunately in our day, we have washing machines. But we still need to keep ourselves just as strong as those women did. Remember that your body is the temple of the Holy Spirit. You need to take care of your body and glorify the Lord with what you put into it and do with it.

It's also important to realize that whenever you are hungry, angry, lonely or tired, you can end up with stress overload. This may lead to a downward spiral that could result in a form of depression. Sometimes, these tend to cluster together. If you are overtired, it's easier to become angry. If you have missed a meal, you are likely to get tired more quickly, and so forth.

So whenever you are feeling too Hungry, too Angry, too Lonely or too Tired, it's time to H.A.L.T. and refocus. Take immediate action by having a healthy bite to eat. Release your anger in prayer, exercise, or an act of reconciliation. Take a nap or go to bed early. It's important to take care of yourself and to know when enough is enough.

There are four areas to concentrate on to stay strong: exercise, proper food, rest, and dealing with stress. As you begin to incorporate these principles into your life, you will step closer to being a more organized woman.

Exercise Every Day

You must move your body every day for energy. Find some form of exercise that you enjoy.

Set exercise goals for yourself:

- Write down why you want to exercise in the first place and tape this to your refrigerator or desk.

- Write out a plan of how you will reach this goal. My goals are to walk every day and work out with light weights.

- Be realistic with your goals. It takes time to get in shape, to get stronger and to lose pounds.

Pick something that is fun. That's why I walk. I really do love it. It can be used as a time to think, pray, and plan as well as a time to be with others. Walk with your husband at night after dinner. Think of all the uninterrupted time you can have with him. Or, walk with your teenager. This can be a great opportunity to spend one on one time with him or her.

Look for activities you can enjoy throughout the year—skiing in the winter, tennis and swimming in the summer. Find activities that make your life full, enriching and alive.

If you have the time and desire, go to a fitness class. Or sign up for tennis, golf or swimming. The rewards of a healthier you are worth the time and effort these may take.

Use your muscles to keep your whole body strong. If you are unable to get outside to exercise, use the stairs in your house: run up and down them. Or exercise to a video tape. Every bit of exercise helps. Even bending down and up when getting something out of a low cabinet, or doing leg lifts while on the telephone, helps to keep you in shape.

Get fit with a friend. I have some friends who work out together in a gym and others who go to Weight Watchers together. Still others meet as a whole group every morning at the school bus stop and walk together after the children leave. They say being together really helps them to stay on course.

Find the right time of day for you to exercise. My husband works out at 6:30 A.M. I could never do that, but that is the best time for him. Once you have picked out the best time for you, stick with it. Once you have exercised for three weeks, it will become a habit.

I know exercising to get in shape can be hard for some people. But I have found that if I do even a little exercise, I really do have more energy. I realized this in a new way during our last blizzard. We couldn't go anywhere because we were snowed in. I had so much fun reading, watching TV, playing with the girls and just being lazy. But by the third day, I didn't feel I had the energy to brush my teeth! I realized the less I do the less energy I have. The next time I'm stuck at home, I'm getting on my treadmill—no excuses!

Eat Properly Every Day for Energy

Food is the fuel our bodies need, and making the right food choices will help keep us going. For some people, losing weight or keeping weight off is almost impossible. I don't mean to minimize that hardship, so I suggest going to a weight-loss professional who could work with you if weight is a substantial problem. The main way to lose weight is by eating less and exercising more, but your body weight can be the sum of many physical and psychological hardships. The tips following are just some basic helps.

Dieting isn't necessary; just concentrate on eating the right foods.

- Stay away from fatty foods and eat plenty of fruits, vegetables and grains.

- Try eating four or five small meals a day instead of one or two larger meals.

- Never skip meals. Your body will try to compensate and will hold on to the food already there.

- Do not eat at fast food restaurants unless you can order something healthy. It's best not to go there at all!

- If you love chocolate or sweets, choose one kind and have a small piece to curb your sweet tooth.

Be aware of high energy foods. These are often quick and convenient, and can keep you going through a hectic day (see sidebar for suggestions from Nancy Clark's *Sports Nutrition Guidebook.* Though these were written by a nutritionist, remember to consider allergies and unique dietary concerns you may have).

Remember as you're going through your day to drink lots of water. We all need at least eight glasses every day. Water helps the

High Energy Foods

1. **Whole grain bagels.** A great source for energy because bagels are complex carbohydrates. They are quick and easy to fix, and great to eat on the run or during those between-meal slumps.

2. **Spinach.** These greens are packed with magnesium. Most women, particularly those who endure stress or strenuous exercise, consume less than optimal levels of this mineral, says Dr. Mildred Seelig, former president of the American College of Nutrition.

3. **Beans.** This food can help with problems of low-level iron deficiencies which cause sluggishness. They are also an excellent substitute for meat for vegetarians. A quick way to eat beans would be a bean soup.

4. **Tuna.** Sometimes called brain food, tuna contains tyrosine, an amino acid. Once digested, tyrosine helps to manufacture brain neurotransmitters which help you perform mental activities. This protein also helps keep your muscles fit and helps you recover after a workout.

5. **Strawberries.** Fruits are a wonderful source of complex carbohydrates. Strawberries are especially rich in vitamin C, which helps your body to absorb iron.

6. **Oatmeal.** A great source of fiber. Fiber helps slow digestion so your body gets a steady stream of energy as carbohydrates gradually flow into your bloodstream. Since this happens gradually, eating oatmeal is much better than a candy bar which gives a fast blast of energy, followed by a quick crash. Hurried mothers like to grab something quick, but you will suffer for not eating right the first time.

7. **Low-fat yogurt.** A great source of calcium which we need for our bones. Researchers now suggest calcium may reduce menstrual cramping and premenstrual water retention by affecting the smooth muscles and hormone secretion.

8. **Bananas.** A great energy snack. The sugars in bananas and other fruits are an easily digested form of carbohydrate. In addition, bananas supply

a heavy dose of potassium, an electrolyte that helps maintain normal muscle and nerve functions, and also helps prevent overheating.

9. **Soybean products.** *Doctors believe that soybean products might cool off those menopausal hot flashes. Soy foods are also loaded with calcium which can battle the bone loss associated with osteoporosis after menopause. Buy some soy milk and make a "smoothie" by blending the soy milk with a little orange juice concentrate and a sliced banana, or pour it on cereal instead of regular milk. Tofu, also a soy product, can be added to soups, stews, and casseroles, or crumbled into spaghetti sauce, soup or a salad. You can also buy crunchy toasted soybean snacks in many supermarkets or soy protein powder to mix with juice.*

condition of your skin, aids digestion, and helps you control your food intake. Carry a water bottle in your car at all times and drink!

Learn to Control the Stress in Your Life

Make time your friend, not your master. Learn to say no to the unimportant and yes to the important.

Learn and practice deep relaxation. Just taking a deep breath can take away some stress. Listen to music when caught in traffic, or use the time to pray instead of fussing about something you can do nothing about. Keep a book in your car or purse so when caught waiting in lines, you can read. Meditate on happy things (Phil. 4:8).

Associate, whenever possible, with gentle people who affirm your personhood. Seek out those people who want your friendship. It took me years to understand this. I would spend time at gatherings with the people who didn't like me because I thought I could change their minds. But, I discovered, being around people who undermine me causes me lots of stress. Now, I seek time with people who care for me.

This principle also works with family members who cause you stress. Be loving and giving to them, but keep your distance when you can. Family gatherings at holidays are good examples of this. Usually, the same disagreements occur each time the extended family gets together. Pray and plan ahead, and avoid those topics or people who start disagreements. By focusing on those you care for the most, the holiday will end better with less stress and deeper bonds formed.

Don't let any one thing dominate your life. Examples include an addiction to watching television, too much time on the computer, or reading novels for hours on end. Balance what you like to do with what you need to do. Our families should always come first.

Free yourself from all dependencies such as addictive relationships, addictive drugs and alcohol, and obsessions of any kind. This is much easier said than done. Go to someone who can help you if you are having trouble in these areas. Christ came to free us: "If the Son makes you free, you will be free indeed" (John 8:36).

Guard your personal freedoms: your choice of friends, your freedom to think and believe as you do, your freedom to structure your time, your freedom to determine your own goals. By this I mean, don't let the opinions of others cause you to change your choices. I care too much about what other people think and I have to remind myself to follow God's will in my life first. (Of course, in a marriage, you should consider your spouse in these decisions, but both of you should love each other enough to allow freedoms.)

Don't allow troublesome relationships and situations to drag you down. Take action: either restore them or end them. Troublesome relationships can really cause a lot of stress. I have had relationships with friends who are just plain hurtful. By ending these, the stress level in my life ended too.

Plan each day carefully, making sure you don't create your own stress by doing too much. Find some time to be alone every day so you can pray, think, and plan. If you don't take care of yourself, you won't be able to care for anyone else.

Get the Rest You Need

It really is true that our bodies need seven to nine hours of sleep every night. If you get this rest, the difference in your energy level and temperament will be remarkable. Mothers are the ones who set the emotional climate for our homes. If we are patient and understanding, our home life will reflect that. But without proper rest, we can become impatient and rude to the very people we love the most.

During the age of the Proverbs woman, when the heat was at its worst, there was a break of activity between noon and three o'clock. This is a wonderful example for us to follow. Try to rest sometime during the day. I get so tired and hungry in the late afternoon that I have a break when my children come home from school. I snack with them and catch up on their day, go over their papers, and review their homework while I get a rest. Besides giving me special time with my children, this break helps me to have the energy for cooking dinner.

But perhaps you are having a hard time getting a good night's sleep. After the birth of my first daughter, I had the hardest time going back to sleep after her middle of the night feeding. This was usually around 4:00 A.M., and to this day, if I wake up at night, it is right around 4:00 A.M. If you're having similar problems, these suggestions may help.

Stick to a bedtime that gives you optimum rest. Deal with worries before you try to sleep. Write down any concerns and troubles with possible solutions and then forget them as you get ready for bed. I even write down things I want my husband to help me with and leave them on the kitchen counter. Then I know he knows the stress I am under and can get these things done.

Avoid caffeine in the late afternoon or after dinner. This isn't just coffee, but cola, tea, and cocoa. Caffeine is a well-known cause of sleeplessness.

Don't use tobacco. Nicotine can cause shallow sleeping.

Have a healthful bedtime snack. Try a small glass of milk and a piece of fruit. Experiments show that people sleep better if they aren't hungry.

Relax. Some people work too hard at getting to sleep. Get in a regular routine at bedtime. Perhaps a ritual of a nightly bath and good book will prepare you for sleep.

> *She senses that her gain is good;*
> *Her lamp does not go out at night.*
> —Proverbs 31:18

The Proverbs woman is a motivated woman. Though she works at having enough rest, she realizes that sometimes, to accomplish the tasks she has to do, she will have to stay up far into the night. One reason she stays up late at night is revealed in verse 24—she is making linen garments and belts to sell. Since she will be earning an income from these, she realizes her gain is good if she works hard at night to finish them.

Sometimes we have to stay up late to finish a project for ourselves or our families. You may remember your own mother staying up at night to finish a costume for you or to help your father pack the car for a long trip. It takes great love and sacrifice to work this hard, but the benefits of meeting your family's needs are rewarding.

Sometimes, it's good to stay up late because there are fewer interruptions. When my children were babies and my husband was traveling, I napped with them in the afternoon. Then after I put them to bed at night, I really got going on projects! One hour at night was more productive than three hours during the day.

If you know you will have to stay up at night to finish a project, try to get some rest during the day. Try not to stay up every night. Our bodies and our dispositions will fade very quickly without the right amount of sleep.

- If you are a morning person, don't stay up at night as the Proverbs woman did. If necessary, get up earlier than usual (it really is still night!) and work then.

- Remember, it takes two days for your body to be affected by more or less sleep. Try to catch back up quickly if you have to stay up late.

The main point to these verses is that the Proverbs woman was always available, physically and mentally, for her family. The lamp of strength, love, and devotion for her family never went out at night.

He gives strength to the weary and increases the power of the weak.   —Isaiah 40:29

Bringing Home Chapter 5

She girds herself with strength
And makes her arms strong.
She senses that her gain is good;
Her lamp does not go out at night.
—Proverbs 31:17–18

Like the Proverbs woman, we must have tremendous energy in order to accomplish everything in our day. It is important to stay healthy so we can achieve our daily goals.

DISCUSSION QUESTIONS

1. Discuss the different ways you exercise. If you don't have time to exercise, what are some alternatives?

2. What type of foods help you to have energy? Is there a time during the day when you like to eat? How could you use this time to make yourself healthier?

3. What causes you the most stress in your life? What could you do to relieve some of it?

4. Are you getting enough rest at night? Are you able to nap or take a short break during the day? If not, how could you add rest to your schedule?

5. Do you have a project you keep putting off? When could you begin this project? (Perhaps you will need to work late once a week to finish it.)

6. What could you add or subtract from your life to make yourself healthier?

PERSONAL APPLICATION

- Review how you exercise, how you eat and how you rest. What could you do differently? Let your answer reflect what would be the best "you" for your family.

6
WORK HARD
AND BE CREATIVE

She looks for wool and flax
And works with her hands in delight.
She stretches out her hands to the distaff,
And her hands grasp the spindle.
                                        —Proverbs 31:13, 19

*T*HESE VERSES ARE descriptions of Hebrew women spinning, turning the wool and the flax into thread. These women were responsible for making all the clothing for the family. The wool came from their own flocks, which they were responsible for taking care of every day. The wool had to be spun into yarn without the use of modern spinning wheels.

The ancient Egyptians and Babylonians were experts in weaving and had large looms, but for the most part the common people of Palestine used a primitive loom and the weaving process was slow and tedious. Of course, there were no sewing machines or steel needles. Their needles were coarse and made of bronze or sometimes of splinters of bone that had been sharpened at one end with a hole at the other end.

This verse also has another meaning. It is the same as saying, "She is never idle," or as the Syrians would say, "Her spindle is never out of her hands." God wants us to realize that idleness is not his desire of how we should live our lives. This Proverbs verse teaches us we need to be busy, productive, and hard workers, especially if we desire to be a more organized woman.

Think back to stories you remember hearing from your grand-mother's and grandfather's early lives. They worked hard! Some were farmers and their day began before sunrise and lasted way after sun-down. Today, many complain when asked to work hard. I would love to see my grandparents' work ethic instilled back into our culture. Billy Graham's book *Just as I Am* gives a great example of this. He shares about his early life working hard on his family's dairy farm:

> I learned to obey without questioning. Lying, cheating, stealing, and property destruction were foreign to me. I was taught that laziness was one of the worst evils, and that there was dignity and honor in labor. I could abandon myself enthusiastically to milking the cows, cleaning out the latrines, and shoveling manure, not because they were pleasant jobs, certainly, but because sweaty labor held its own satisfaction.

Think about the type of tremendously hard work most women have had to do in the past. Household helps such as washing machines, vacuum cleaners, indoor plumbing and water have just been in use in the last hundred years. Before that, women had to do everything by hand. In the days of the Proverbs 31 woman, she was responsible for the grinding of the grain each morning and it often required half a day to complete. She had to do the cooking, weave the cloth, and make the clothes. She had to take care of the flocks where she would get the wool for the cloth, and she also was respon-sible for caring for the goats. Washing clothes took a great amount of time for she had to go to the nearest source of water and dip and beat the clothes with a club. The women were also the ones who had to go to the well or spring for the household water and the water for the animals. They carried pitchers of water on their head, shoulders or hips. This was heavy and time-consuming work.

And, of course, she had to take care of her babies and children, and manage the upkeep and cleaning of the home. I don't know if I would have survived back in those days! These women never had to drive carpools or go to P.T.A. meetings, but they faced illness, death, and starvation on a regular basis. Let us look at our work loads with thankfulness for all the modern helps we have.

There are many Proverbs written on the benefits of hard work. Here are two to remember:

- Lazy people are soon poor; hard workers get rich (Proverbs 10:4 NLT).

- Work hard and become a leader; be lazy and become a slave (Proverbs 12;24 NLT).

May you think of the Proverbs woman and view your home and work load as thread on a loom that needs to be woven together. "Stretch out your hand" to every area of your home, "grasp" what needs to be done and keep it going. Here are some tips for the task at hand.

Work Productively

Begin to view your work at home and your work outside the home as important. As our attitudes change toward the positive, we will have more energy and desire to work hard at whatever we have to do.

Try always to have at least one enjoyable home project or personal project. This will help keep you motivated, for you will finish what has to be done faster to get to what you *want* to do. The old saying is true: "Ask the person to help you who is the busiest person you know." The more we have to do, the more we are able to get done. Of course, too much to do can have the opposite effect and you won't get anything done at all. Balance is the key here. Think of the things you have always wanted to do or make but never thought you had the time or talents for. Narrow this list down to one thing and do it.

Do your chores first thing every day. Part of working hard is starting the day productively. You will never get behind because you will be using your energy level on what has to be done. Then you will have time to do what you would like to do.

Express Your Creativity

Hard work is important, but you also need to *enjoy* the life you live. That is where creativity comes in. The Proverbs woman "works with her hands in delight" (Prov. 31:13). How can you turn your daily homemaking job more fulfilling, enjoyable and delightful? How can you imbue work outside the home with real purpose in your life?

Start with your attitude. View your life and the work you do in it as a gift from God. "Whatever you do, work at it with all your heart, as working for the Lord, not for men, since you know that you will receive an inheritance from the Lord as a reward. It is the Lord Christ you are serving" (Col. 3:23–24).

Look at your jobs and responsibilities in a new way. Use your creativity to turn any difficult chore into a special memory.

- Do you have to visit your sick grandmother in the nursing home? Take a game for you two to play or take her outside for a picnic.

- Do you need to clean out the garage? Turn a difficult chore into a fun learning time by asking your younger child to count everything the two of you take out of the garage.

- Do you dislike going to the grocery store? Plan to stop at your favorite deli when you're done shopping; pick up a great sandwich as a reward.

Plan one day a week or one event a week that you can look forward to. Having something to anticipate can really be motivating and can help keep your spirits up. Being creative can add a special dimension to life.

Rethink what you want to do with your life. Make a list of everything you wish to accomplish or experience. Include your dreams.

- What hobbies would you like to pursue?
- What new things would you like to experience or try?
- What do you find really fun? What makes you happy?
- What have you been putting off that you would feel better about if you completed? Or started?
- Would you want to study again? How about art, a new language, or a cooking class?
- What could you do to be more creative with your health, body, level of fitness and sense of well-being?

Be creative with your future. What things have you done in the past that have brought you joy and meaning in your life and how can you continue them into the future?

Be creative with your emotions. Quit allowing your negative emotions to get the better of you, and show positive and joyful emotions to your family and to yourself. Did you wake up in a bad mood? Purpose to change the bad mood and be happy to see your family. On a rainy day, find one thing that's sunny and concentrate on it. Allow yourself to love and to be loved.

Ask yourself how you could be more creative in each area of your life: in your home, in your relationships, in your personal life. This might seem a little overwhelming, but part of becoming a more organized woman is thinking of ways you can improve every area of your life. Ask God to help you in this process.

Consider a craft project or adding something beautiful to your home. Take a look at one of the many magazines that offer ideas on how to be creative in your home, your yard, and your kitchen. *Martha Stewart's Living* is one good example. There are also many craft and hobby shops (such as Hobby Lobby and Michael's) that can give you ideas. Many of these stores also have classes you can take to learn a new craft. Walk through your home with paper and pen and write down ideas of how you can organize each room or how you can creatively make it into your home.

- Make a wreath with silk flowers to go over your fireplace. Or put together a vase of dried flowers for the hallway. Another idea is to make decorations for your front door that match whatever season you're in. I have four different arrangements for our front door and I love changing them as the seasons change.

- If sewing is a way you want to express your creativity, make curtains for the kitchen or drapes for the living room.

- If you don't have the money or time for a large sewing project, make and furnish a small doll house for your daughter. That way, you are teaching her to be creative and to use her talents while having fun yourself.

- Make a quilt. I always wanted to do this, but never thought I could do an entire quilt. But I've discovered a sewing store where I can buy one square a month, beginning in January and ending in December. After I finish making the last square, I'll have enough for one quilt! Remember, a quilt can make a lovely wall hanging.

- Hand sew cross-stitching and make beautiful pictures or verses that could be framed for your home or for presents.

- Begin a collection of some kind and showcase it. I have a friend who began collecting tea cups some years ago.

Because many of us knew about her collection, she often received a tea cup for birthdays, anniversaries and Christmas. Each cup is different. My friend had a lighted cabinet made to display this beautiful and unique collection. Other people collect antiques, dolls, or miniatures. There are many choices about what to collect, which is what makes this particular project so expressive.

- Use plants to express your creativity. Plants can easily change an ordinary room into a warm and inviting one. Visit a local nursery and talk to the staff. They'll have wonderful ideas of the type of plants that would work best in your home and for your climate. (Philodendron is one species that works well anywhere and is hard to kill.)

Every one of us can be creative, even if we don't think we can be. There are hundreds of possibilities for making our homes more beautiful and personal. That's really one of the end results as we strive to become more organized women. As our lives become more organized and balanced, we are able to go to the next step: making our lives more beautiful.

Ask God to give you the strength to work hard and the ability to be creative in every area of your life. Focus on the beautiful instead of the mundane, and you'll move from existing to really living!

Every skilled woman spun with her hands and brought what she had spun—blue, purple or scarlet yarn or fine linen, and all the women who were willing and had the skill spun the goat hair. . . . Then Moses said . . . See, the Lord . . . has filled him with the spirit of God, with skill, ability and knowledge in all kind of crafts.   —Exodus 35: 25–26, 31

Bringing Home Chapter 6

She looks for wool and flax
And works with her hands in delight.
She stretches out her hands to the distaff,
And her hands grasp the spindle.
                                    —Proverbs 31:13, 19

Part of the joy in life is finding things we like to do. The Proverbs woman was creative and enjoyed working with her hands. But as verse 19 says, she wasn't lazy. She worked hard. Being more creative in the home and focusing on what God says about hard work are fruitful tasks.

DISCUSSION QUESTIONS

1. In what areas of your life could you change from being somewhat lazy to being more hard working?
2. How important do you feel your attitude is as you go about your household chores? Do you "work with your hands in delight"?
3. What do you want to accomplish in your life? On a smaller scale, what hobbies or activities would you like to start doing now?
4. Name one craft project that you might enjoy doing. What supplies do you need to get started on it?

PERSONAL APPLICATION

- Go through your home, either mentally or physically, and ask yourself, "How could I work harder or more efficiently? How could I use creative ideas in my home to make it a haven for myself and for my family?"

She extends her hand to the poor,
And she stretches out her hands to the needy.
—Proverbs 31:20

HE PROVERBS WOMAN realizes she needs to think of the less fortunate. This requirement is implicit in Jesus' commandment that we love and support the needy in all walks of life. He said, "Inasmuch as ye have done it unto one of the least of these my brethren, ye have done it unto me" (Matt. 25:40 KJV). The Proverbs woman is an example for women today, reminding us to help others in need. This isn't just for the poor, but for that neighbor who is sick and needs a meal, or that family member who needs help. The needy may be anyone anywhere who needs our help. And because of the many needy people in life, the need to be organized becomes more important. (We have to be organized in our own life so we can reach out to others.)

To see how this verse applies to our life, look at the way people lived in Biblical times. Reaching out to others, showing hospitality, was a great honor for the people of this time. They believed a person who becomes their guest is sent to them by God. Thus, hospitality, or reaching out to someone needy, became a sacred duty. When Abraham entertained three strangers who proved to be angels, he showed an attitude of great joy. He "ran to meet" the three men, he "hastened into the tent unto Sarah" to get her to make ready food, he "ran unto the herd" and then he "fetched a calf . . . and hastened to dress it" (Gen. 18:2, 6–7 KJV).

Centuries later, the writer of Hebrews agreed with this thought. "Be not forgetful to entertain strangers: for thereby some have entertained angels unawares" (Heb. 13:2 KJV). Paul also exhorted the Roman believers to "share with God's people who are in need. Practice hospitality" (Rom. 12:13 NIV).

During the persecutions of early Christians, such hospitality could save lives. How welcome a home of refuge would be to one who had to flee his own home. Hospitality among the early Christians promoted fellowship, and thus strengthened growth in the faith. It must have also been a great influence upon the youth growing up in the homes where helping those in need was practiced.

These examples of hospitality show us how God wants us to live. We Christian women need to recognize that there are many poor people in this world. In biblical times, the poor were more obvious. The Proverbs woman passed the poor daily as she walked to the market. Today, most of the world's poor are located in our cities and in third world countries. Although we might not pass by them in our day-to-day activities, we should still be aware that some people, including whole families, suffer great need. We must do whatever we can to help them. As Christ said, the poor will always be with us. But we can make the choice of "extending our hand to the poor." Our schedules should never be so busy that we cannot stop and be there for others.

As God causes you to feel a burden for others, don't allow the tremendous needs to overwhelm you. Instead, pray for wisdom and begin with one small step. Each of us has a different circle of influence and individual ability to help those around us. If each one of us does our small part, needy people will be helped.

Many times the plight of the impoverished does overwhelm me. Have you ever shut off a newscast in mid-program because the world's problems were too much for you to bear that day? I am forced once again to realize I can't possibly do everything I want for others and my family. Once again, in order to do all I can, I must be organized—even to the point of categorizing people by my priorities. This concept may sound cold, but it is not; it simply means my family comes first, then others. If I helped strangers so much my family rarely saw me, that would be wrong. By organizing my time, I can sometimes help others without neglecting my family

As I've prayed through this issue, I've come up with the following priorities for who I believe I should help first, and how much. May it stimulate you to prayerfully form your own priorities of whom God wants you to serve.

Reach Out to Your Family

This includes my husband and children. I am to take care of their needs before anyone else's. It is difficult to say no to people, but if I take care of my family first, I'll be able to care for others better. It would be a shame to volunteer so much I don't have time to cook my own family dinner. There are exceptions, however. Taking care of someone sick, helping a family move into a new house, or helping in an emergency are situations that sometimes come first.

Next in the family category are my mother and father, grandmothers and grandfathers, sisters and brothers, in-laws, cousins, nieces and nephews.

Try to remember birthdays and anniversaries. Call when you can or write letters if you live out of town from them.

Be available for family dinners or get-togethers. Your extended family should be an important part of your life.

When a need comes up, rally around that family member and do all you can to help, especially the sick, the aged, and those with

STEP 7: REACH OUT TO THE NEEDY

financial problems. Elderly parents who become sick and helpless are a severe problem for their middle-aged children. These children are called the sandwich generation because they are caught between their children who need them and their aged parents who need them. The exhaustion and helplessness they feel can be overwhelming. This would be the time to go to your pastor or others for help. Remember to pray. God will give you the strength to get through it.

Reach Out to Your Friends

I am very loyal to my friends. I want to be there for them as much as I possibly can. Friends are people who also have illnesses, family troubles, and hardships. We need to be available to stretch out our hand to them in their need. If you don't have the time in your life now to help a friend, then maybe you are doing too much. What could you change in your life?

If friends are sick, be ready to help with a drive to the doctor or to pick up something at the store. Keep a meal frozen in your freezer so you will have one to give away quickly if a friend is in need.

Be available to talk to them when they need you, in person or by phone. Try to stop what you are doing and be sure to listen well. Many times all a friend needs is someone to listen and to care. Have empathy—put yourself in their shoes. Offer encouragement. Don't nag or argue.

E-mail them a short message so they know you care. That way you don't need to spend too much time on the telephone.

Accept your friends as they are. Praise their accomplishments and never be jealous of them. Be forgiving. And if you need to, don't be afraid to say you're sorry.

Always keep promises and secrets. Never gossip.

Reach Out to Your Neighbors

If you're blessed, your neighbors are already your friends. For most of us, some are, and some are not. But what a great opportunity to reach others for Christ! Your neighborhood can be your mission field. You don't have to go to some far-off country to have a mission. The harvest for bringing people to Christ is ripe all over the world. Reach out to your neighbors whenever your can. Witness by action.

Remember, even though your neighbors may live in nice homes, the outside of the buildings can camouflage hurts and needs inside. Be a missionary in your neighborhood; reach out to the needy right there.

If your neighbor just had an operation, take over a meal.

If your neighbors tell you they are going out of town, offer to pick up their mail for them.

If their children are alone after school, see if you can have them over some afternoons. Reach out to neighborhood children by being kind and interested in them. Often you don't know what kind of home they come from. Your love and caring might be the only attention they get.

Invite your neighbors to your church or your church's special programs. Some of my friends invite the neighborhood children to our AWANA program. Many of these parents don't have a church, but they begin to come when they see the enthusiasm of their children.

Reach Out in Your Community and Church

This is the area of my life that includes my children's schools, community affairs, and our church. If you are interested in helping in one of these areas, here are some suggestions.

Find out what organizations help the poor and homeless in your town or city. You can help support them financially. You can also work in areas of need such as soup kitchens or daycare centers.

Volunteer at the schools, in the classrooms, at special events, or for the PTA.

Help with clean-up programs such as "adopt-a-highway." Plant trees and flowers, or pick up litter.

Help at your local community center. Contact the Chamber of Commerce and ask for areas that need help.

Volunteer at a nursing home or adopt a needy group. One school in our town helps a housing project for single parent families. The sixth grade students collect household items, children's toys, diapers, and clothes for these families. They also collect money for these needs by having a fundraiser at Wendy's. The students advertise the night, encouraging the community to eat at Wendy's. The students work during the event, clearing tables and getting drinks for the customers. Sometimes the night has a theme, such as Fifties Night. Wendy's donates part of their profits from the night to the project.

Join an organization such as the Junior League. These groups always need volunteers for their many programs focused on the poor.

Find out the needs at your local church:

- Are there single parents in the church? One of the greatest problems they face is the overwhelming amount of work to be done. Maybe your husband could help with a plumbing problem or you could type a resumé.

- Organize a special bulletin board at church listing people's needs, as well as people who can help. Then people would have a way of knowing and meeting a specific need.

- Help organize emergency food or rent support for people who are struggling.

- Help sort used clothing for your church's clothes closet, or stock and distribute food for the food pantry.

- Become a friend to the pastors and the staff at your church and help them whenever you can. They are under a tremendous strain every day trying to meet the never-ending needs of their congregation and community.

- Pray for your community, your schools and your church. Ask God to help them and to help you know how you can reach out to others.

Paul in Ephesians 6:18–19 asked for prayer:

> And pray in the Spirit on all occasions with all kinds of prayers and requests. With this in mind, be alert and always keep on praying for all the saints. Pray also for me, that whenever I open my mouth, words may be given me so that I will fearlessly make known the mystery of the gospel. (NIV)

Reach Out in Your City, State and Country

Helping with the needy in a large city and state can be difficult. But most cities have soup kitchens, homeless shelters, daycare centers or foster child programs.

Volunteer as a guide at a museum, as a pink lady at a hospital, or as a reading mentor at a library. Volunteer your time to build homes through Habitat for Humanity, or help financially.

Contact your representatives in Washington, D.C. and find out ways that you can help the needy in the country. The United States of America, is the strongest, richest, and freest country in the world. One important way we all can help is to remember to pray for our country and our governing officials. In fact, Paul exhorts us to pray for them in 1 Timothy 2:1–2:

> First of all, then, I urge that entreaties and prayers, petitions and thanksgivings, be made on behalf of all men, for kings and all who are in authority, so that we may lead a tranquil and quiet life in all godliness and dignity.

Be sure to vote! Your vote can make a difference. What you believe in and how you want your officials to make decisions is shown when you vote. Sometimes people quit voting, believing one vote doesn't make a difference. But one vote can make a difference. In 1960 John F. Kennedy won (and Richard Nixon lost) the presidential election by a margin of less than one vote per precinct nationwide.

Write letters and voice your opinions. Make your voice heard in every level of your government. As an old saying goes, "The only thing it takes for evil to win is for good people to do nothing."

Support organizations who believe as you do and are working to help preserve our freedoms. Many Christian organizations work tirelessly for our country's youth and families. Focus on the Family in Colorado Springs, Colorado, is one example of an organization that strives to protect the rights and freedoms of families. Passage of legislation that would have been devastating to families was stopped because Focus on the Family worked hard to inform people. Some of us feel it's too hard to keep up with politics and too uncomfortable to think about all the evil that is going on in our country. However, we need to be just as compassionate and forceful about our freedoms as our forefathers were who died for those freedoms and for us.

Reach Out to Our World

Reaching out to the world's needy can be an overwhelming task. However, there are hundreds of organizations and thousands of people already reaching out who you can support.

Support the missionaries from your church with finances, gifts and prayers.

Check out organizations who give help to the world's poor and give to them. The Red Cross, World Vision, Billy Graham Relief, and the 700 Club are but a few of the organizations who send tremendous aid to millions of people.

"Adopt-a-Child." Ministries like World Vision or Compassion International are available to support children in many different countries all over the world with your small, monthly fee. Our family supports one child in Africa, and my teenager, with some of her youth

group friends, helps support another. Today we can help people struggling with poverty, one child at a time.

If you think just one person cannot make a difference, think about the lifelong ministry of one woman, Mother Teresa. She began her ministry in 1948 by lifting up one dying man and helping him. Today, in less than fifty years, her missionaries operate in over one hundred countries, with about four thousand members. Each year, the charity feeds 500,000 families, teaches over 40,000 slum children, treats almost 100,000 leprosy patients, and operates AIDS shelters, homes for abandoned children, houses for recovering alcoholics, shelters for abused women and the destitute, and conducts disaster relief in some of the most unlikely places in the world.

God knows that we can make a difference in other people's lives. He gave us the example of Proverbs 31:20 to encourage us to reach out to others, beginning with our own families and extending into the world. Remember that when Christ was on the earth, he didn't heal everyone or take poverty away. He did the work God sent him here to do, just as we can only do what God has for us. Pray and ask God where he wants you to help.

"Let your light shine before men in such a way that they may see your good works, and glorify your Father who is in heaven."
— Matthew 5:16

Bringing Home Chapter 7

She extends her hand to the poor;
And she stretches out her hands to the needy.
—Proverbs 31:20

The Proverbs woman realizes that she needs to think of the less fortunate. As Christ said, "What you do for the least of these, you are doing to me" (Matt. 25:45). The Proverbs woman is a wonderful example for women today, reminding us to help others in need. This isn't just for the poor, but for that neighbor who is sick and needs a meal, or for that family member who needs help.

DISCUSSION QUESTIONS

1. Who do you think the needy are?
2. What organizations do you know of that help the needy in your area? Which ones would you want to work with?
3. How can you help others without feeling overwhelmed or neglecting your family?
4. What are some ways you can help your friends, neighbors or community?
5. What types of ministries does your church have, and how could you help with them?

PERSONAL APPLICATION

- Prayerfully select a need and decide to help in this area for the next year. This could be a personal commitment or a family activity.

8

MANAGE YOUR
CLOTHES AND CLOSETS

She is not afraid of the snow for her household,
For all her household are clothed with scarlet.
She makes coverings for herself;
Her clothing is fine linen and purple.
Strength and dignity are her clothing,
And she smiles at the future.

—Proverbs 31:21–22, 25

LOTHES. We can't live without them. But they do take a lot of time and effort. Eve had it easy until she ate that apple!

Now don't get me wrong. I love clothes. I love to wear something new, to have accessories that really complement an outfit, to have new shoes and to look the best I can. However, there is one problem: I don't like to shop. So taking care of my family's clothing needs is hard for me. I usually catalogue shop for myself, which can be fast and simple. But to keep up with the clothes my family needs takes more time and effort—which brings us to the verses above.

The Proverbs woman was organized in taking care of her family's clothing needs. She wasn't afraid of bad weather because her whole household was well taken care of in advance.

Since I live in Denver, this verse makes complete sense to me. The weather seems to change every fifteen minutes here. We have to be prepared for a sudden snowfall as early as August. So, as soon as the children start back to school, I start pulling out all our gloves, snow boots, hats, and coats to see if replacements need to be bought. I have a plastic bin placed on the shelves in my laundry room for each person in the family, and this is where their gloves, hats, sunglasses, and goggles go. Then, when we need them, everyone knows where they are and we don't panic when that first snow comes.

"Clothed in scarlet" is a reference to the time the Proverbs woman devoted to clothing her family. The Proverbs woman had to spend a lot of time and energy dyeing material scarlet before even making clothes. For all of her family to be clothed in scarlet meant one of her priorities was dressing her family the very best she could.

"Her clothing is fine linen and purple" reveals that she showed her beauty with simplicity, not a display of silks and jewels. Fine linen took more work to weave than other fabrics. It was not coarse, and had great beauty. In her day, purple was royalty's color.

There is no sin in being the best we can be for God and our family. We should glorify God in every area of life. This requires a balanced approach, for in 1 Peter 3:3 it says, "your adornment must not be merely external—braiding the hair, and wearing gold jewelry . . ." Peter wasn't forbidding women from styling their hair or wearing jewelry at all; he just didn't want women to be preoccupied with those things, as they were in Roman society. Peter was saying that we need a healthy balance in our lives, as the Proverbs woman had.

When I was a little girl, my mother made just about everything my sisters and I wore. I remember coming home after school and seeing my mother and my grandmother going through all the clothes that had been stored away. They let out hems or took up hems from hand-me-downs. It was a great way to save money but it also showed me the value in reusing clothing. My mother and grandmother taught me, by their hard work ethic, how to take care of clothes. They were an example for me when I began to take care of my children's clothes. We never left the house without looking clean and well taken care of, from our shoes up to how our hair looked. Mother helped us develop a good self-image because of the time and effort she put into helping us look our best.

This is an important point. It does take a tremendous amount of time and effort to have your children look their best. But these verses help us see that this is an important area to put your time. As you become more organized in your home and life, you'll find the extra time to keep up with their clothes and hair and will also have the time to show your children how to take care of themselves as they get older.

Most working mothers today barely have time to look in their children's closet to see what is there, much less have time to sew. But the more involved a mother can be in her young children's clothes, the more money she can save and the better-dressed the child will be.

The Proverbs woman didn't pick just any fabric, she looked until she found quality products. Flax was used for making linen which was lighter for the warmer seasons and was used for the more beautiful clothing. Wool was used for colder climates. To sew with wool, she had to care for the sheep, remove the wool, make the thread, make the cloth, dye the cloth and finally make the garment. She had to put forth tremendous effort to clothe all her household.

We, too, need to put forth effort and time if our household will be clothed correctly. Below are some tips on sorting, storing, buying, and cleaning your clothes. As you read these tips, remember that taking care of your family's clothes is another step toward becoming a more organized woman.

Develop a Method for Sorting and Storing Clothes

Twice a year, exchange a season of clothes in your closets and drawers. In late summer or early fall, pull out all the summer items, sort them, and place them in storage. In early spring, remove the heavy winter items from your closet and replace them with the spring and summer ones. When I remove a season from a closet, I put the clothes in five piles:

- Laundry
- Dry cleaners
- Mending
- Give away
- Ready to be stored

Make a habit of regularly going through your young children's closets and drawers to straighten and organize. You will be able to see if more clothes are needed, and what needs cleaning or mending. When my children were younger, I sometimes found dirty clothes back on their shelves. I discovered I needed to regularly check their closets. By keeping up on their closets and drawers, the twice-a-year switch from one season to another was not as difficult. As your children get older, teach them to become responsible in this same way.

Get rid of clothes that you haven't worn in three years. There are many people who are in real need of clothes. We should be willing to give clothes we don't use to others who would use them. This will also help to keep our closets streamlined and organized.

Go through all your stockings, belts, accessories, and jewelry to throw out old items and to reorganize the rest. Store the items you retain where you can find them at a moment's notice, fresh and ready. I place my hose, still packaged, vertically in a small box in my closet. Each package is labeled with the color of hose, so I can quickly find the pair I want. After wearing, I file the hose back in the same package and back in the box. This suggestion may seem silly, but even this little bit of organization simplifies my life.

Organize your belts on a hanger or buy a belt rack for your closet. If you or your daughters use hair bows, you can clip them to a cloth belt and hang the belt on a hook or coat hanger. Then your bows are all in a beautiful, rainbow-colored line and you can find the color you want quickly.

Buy plastic or cardboard storage bins to help organize out-of-season clothes. These can be placed on shelves or under a bed. These containers are also wonderful for storing prized heirlooms such as baby clothes.

Avoid plastic dry-cleaning bags for long term storage. They trap moisture and encourage mildew. Instead, use fabric clothing bags or acid-free cardboard boxes, or cover clothing with old sheets.

Add blocks of cedar, boxes of scented candles or old perfume bottles to the closet to keep clothes smelling fresh. You can also tuck sweet-smelling sachets between clothes in closets and drawers.

At the end of the day, before putting your clothes away in a tightly packed closet, hang them where they can air out.

Buy hooks for every thing and every place you need to organize. They are wonderful for the backs of bathroom and closet doors, and in the laundry room for coats and backpacks. Keep things off the floor and on shelves and hooks. Your home will look less cluttered and more open.

Buy an inexpensive cardboard cabinet with drawers for your closet to keep lingerie, socks, or accessories organized.

Buy closet expanders. This will increase how much your closet holds. These can be bought at most discount or building supply stores. Another possibility is to hire a company such as California Closet to come to your home and redesign your closets. You will be amazed at the extra space you will have. It's well worth the price.

Have a specific drawer, shelf or hook for each item. If you always keep your swimsuits, nightgowns, sweaters and belts in the same place, you will be able to find what you need when you want it. You won't lose things as easily and you'll have less clutter.

Invest in better quality hangers. These are well worth the bit of extra money you'll spend. They make your closet look better, too.

- Use the larger plastic, colored hangers for most items. Your clothes will not be pressed as close together in the closet as with wire hangers, so they will look better and need less re-ironing.

- Hang delicate garments on padded hangers whenever possible.

- Invest in buying pant hangers. Your pants will hang higher on the rod, leaving more space on the shelf or on the floor below for other storage.

Fold sweaters and store them on shelves or in drawers.

Don't forget your hall closet! Sort through the winter coats and jackets each spring and clean them, store them or give them away. If you store cameras and equipment on the shelf in this closet, buy plastic bins to organize. Add extra hangers for guest's coats.

Buy Clothes Wisely

The best time to buy new clothes is after you have sorted and stored away the clothes in your closets. You'll see what you need to replace or what you need to buy for the new season. Write down what each person in the family needs and your buying trip will go more quickly.

Be on the lookout for sales. Buy winter coats in January. Buy jeans and play clothes at discount stores. Stores such as Target, Mervyn's, and Wal-Mart are a great source for basic family clothing needs such as gloves, hats, shirts, camp clothes, and swimming suits. The prices are usually much lower than at department stores and the quality is fine for children who are growing.

Though sales are wonderful, don't buy something just because it is on sale. Make sure you need the item. It is better to have one great outfit than a closet full of sale items you don't wear or need.

As your children get older, let them help you with their clothing purchases. Make shopping a fun outing! Let your children know that taking care of them is a joy and that their opinion about what they wear is important to you.

Let your children have a clothing allowance. Then they can be responsible for the cost and the choices of their own clothes. This will be a great tool in teaching them money management.

If you enjoy sewing, make some of your family's clothes. This can help greatly with the finances. I love needlework, so I smocked dresses for my two daughters when they were little. It saved money on expensive dresses and my daughters remember me making them something special. The dresses will be heirlooms for them to keep.

Develop an Efficient Method for Keeping Clothes Clean

Taking care of the clothes you already have is important if you want to be a good steward of your money and possessions. Your favorite clothes will also last longer if you take good care of them.

Wash clothes on a regular basis. You don't want clothes to sit in heaps growing mildew. Pretreat stains as soon as you can.

Follow directions for your washer and dryer exactly. Select the best water temperature for each load. Always sort wash loads by color and fabric type. Although my white towels could be washed in my white loads, I keep towels separate from my regular clothes. This keeps the clothes from being overwashed and they won't dry as hot as if they were dried with towels. Never overload your washer or dryer. It can damage your machines and your clothes will not get as clean.

Remove your clothes from the dryer before it stops. This reduces wrinkles. Another good tip: Let your knit shirts stay in the dryer for only a few minutes. Take them out while still damp, and hang them up on a wide hanger to dry. Smooth out wrinkles, and when they're dry they won't need any ironing.

Always dry on the lowest heat setting, except with towels. For towels, use the medium setting. The high setting can damage your clothes.

Keep your laundry area neat by using shelves and hooks. Keep a trash can there for the lint you remove from the dryer. Have special bins for different type of clothes to be washed: one for whites, one for darks, one for towels, and one for delicate or hand-washed items. Your goal is to keep these bins empty.

Have a special rod or hook for clothes that need ironing. Then, have one set time each week to iron. I like to iron while I watch TV newscasts. I have a portable ironing board I place on the kitchen counter. Before I realize it, all my ironing is finished.

Having said all that, remember what Jesus said about clothing in Matthew 6:28–29:

> "And why are you worried about clothing? Observe how the lilies of the field grow; they do not toil nor do they spin, yet I say to you that not even Solomon in all his glory clothed himself like one of these."

Though taking care of our family's clothing needs is important, there are others things that are more important. "Strength and dignity are her clothing" (Prov. 31:25). Instead of focusing completely on our clothes, we should be concerned with the beauty of our character. We should hope that our inner qualities are obvious to anyone who is with us. The Proverbs woman had this inner strength and dignity that was seen by others. She knew who was in charge of her life: the Lord. She had an eternal view of life instead of a temporal one. So, she could smile at the future because she knew her life and the lives of her family were in the hands of God.

Your beauty should not come from outward adornment, such as braided hair and the wearing of gold jewelry and fine clothes. Instead, it should be that of your inner self, the unfading beauty of a gentle and quiet spirit, which is of great worth in God's sight. —1 Peter 3:3–4 NIV

Bringing Home Chapter 8

She is not afraid of the snow for her household,
For all her household are clothed with scarlet.
She makes coverings for herself;
Her clothing is fine linen and purple.
Strength and dignity are her clothing,
And she smiles at the future.
                                    —Proverbs 31:21–22, 25

Taking care of your family's clothes and clothing your family well is important.

DISCUSSION QUESTIONS

1. What is the hardest part about keeping up with your family's clothes?
2. What ideas do you have for sorting and storing your clothes?
3. Where do you buy most of the clothes for you and your family?
4. Do you have any special tips on cleaning and caring for your clothes?
5. Is there anything you could do differently so that your family's clothes appear their very best?

PERSONAL APPLICATION

- What could you do personally so that your inner character is more beautiful than your outward appearance?

9

NURTURE
YOUR CHILDREN

She opens her mouth in wisdom,
And the teaching of kindness is on her tongue.
—Proverbs 31:26

NOTHING IN THIS WORLD gives us more joy than our children, and nothing takes as much time and energy! God looks at children as precious gifts: "Behold, children are a gift of the LORD; the fruit of the womb is a reward" (Ps. 127:3). Jesus himself rebuked the disciples when they tried to make a group of children go away:

> Then some children were brought to Him so that He might lay His hands on them and pray; and the disciples rebuked them. But Jesus said, "Let the children alone, and do not hinder them from coming to Me; for the kingdom of heaven belongs to such as these."   —Matthew 19:13–14

Proverbs 31:26 offers us an example of how to treat children. We need to open our mouths in wisdom, not with constant criticism and put-downs, and to teach and talk to our children with kindness, not with yelling and harsh words.

Proverbs 31:1 shows us that King Lemuel learned prophecy from his mother. In 2 Timothy 3:15, Paul said to Timothy, "From childhood you have known the sacred writings." Timothy had been taught by his mother and grandmother, as most Hebrew children were in biblical days. Daughters remained under their mother's guidance and teaching until their marriage. Sons were taught more and more by their fathers and their local rabbi as they grew up, but they also continued to be taught by their mothers.

The duty of educating the children was commanded by the Mosaic law. The home became the classroom:

> "And these words, which I am commanding you today, shall be on your heart. You shall teach them diligently to your sons and shall talk of them when you sit in your house and when you walk by the way and when you lie down and when you rise up" (Deut. 6:6–7).

This is a well-quoted verse instructing Jewish parents to consistently teach their children every day about the Lord and his law. We should be just as diligent in training our children.

These examples show that we, too, can be teachers to our children and have "kindness" on our tongue. As Paul instructed in Ephesians 4:32, "Be kind to one another, tender-hearted." We should begin this instruction with our own precious children. As we begin to organize our children's lives, it will help us step closer to that goal of becoming a more organized woman.

The following tips can help you organize all aspects of life with your children so you can be there for them. However, these are tips, not commandments. Don't let all these suggestions overwhelm you until you don't want to try anything. Choose the tips you feel God wants you to use with your family.

Take Time to Read with Your Children

One of my most important goals in raising my children is to have at least thirty minutes every night to read with them. I guard this goal with my life! I have given up television and numerous activities to be home with them at night.

"Reading Literacy in the United States," a 1996 study, found compelling evidence that parents make a difference in their child's reading achievement. Fourth grade average reading scores were forty-six points below the national average where principals judged parental involvement to be low, but twenty points above the national average where parental involvement was high. This is simple to do, and it's free. Besides, children love it! Reading to your children every night requires turning the television off, but parenting requires sacrifices. If you are not quite sure how to start reading to your child, here are some tips from the Jefferson County Schools Communications Services.

Read to your child every day, even to tiny babies. Point to the pictures and say the names of the various objects. Point to the printed word as you read aloud. This will help them understand that words on a page have meaning, that words go from left to right, that letters make up words, and that letters have small and capital sizes.

As they begin to read for themselves, continue your reading with them. This is a great time to read them the classics and to expose them to different people and cultures.

Take them to the library. Get them their own library card. Have magazines and books available to them.

Be an example by letting your children see you read. Turn off the television and spend the evening with a good book. Talk about what you have been reading.

Talk to your children about what they are reading at home and at school. Help them decide on books for their book reports.

Play word and rhyming games. Between the ages of four and seven, most children begin to recognize words. They can read signs to you from the car. Ask them about the sounds of the letters in the words they are reading.

Encourage your child to write about what she has read. She could even keep a journal of the titles and authors of the books.

Continue reading to your children as long as they will let you. I was able to read to my oldest daughter until she was in the eighth grade of middle school. One night she said she was old enough to do her Bible and story readings by herself. I was proud of her and knew it was time for her to start, even though it made me sad.

Take Time to Nurture Your Child's Spiritual Life

Keep a basket by your children's rocking chair or bed filled with devotional books you want to read to them. Before you read the usual bedtime story, start with one of the devotional stories. My children have never complained about our devotional time because they thought we were just reading books.

Here are some of the devotional books I've used and my daughters have enjoyed. Kenneth N. Taylor has written some wonderful books such as *The Bible in Pictures for Little Eyes, Big Thoughts for Little People,* and *Giant Steps for Little People.* These books are excellent for children up to ages seven or eight. Another wonderful devotional book is *The Beginners Bible—Timeless Children's Stories. Little Visits with God* by Jahsmann and Simon is a collection of everyday stories with a moral in each one.

For an older child, *The One Year Bible Storybook* by Virginia J. Muir is an excellent book for daily devotions. Each day of the year has a designated reading beginning with Genesis for January 1 and ending with the book of Revelation in December.

Don't forget faith-oriented magazines. A great source of material for children is Focus on the Family. Both our girls receive magazines according to their ages: *Clubhouse* for my nine year old, and *Brio* for my teenager. The excellent articles are appropriate for growing kids.

Focus on the Family also offers *Adventures in Odyssey,* fabulous audio tapes which we take on our car trips. These tapes have influenced the character of my children. You can also hear the Odyssey series on local Christian radio stations. My daughter likes to hear an episode before she goes to sleep. Focus on the Family has many more video tapes and books. Check with your local Christian bookstore, or call Focus on the Family directly at: 1-800-A-Family.

Spend fifteen to thirty minutes of time with each child before they go to sleep. Reading to them, talking to them, and praying with them is a valuable way to nurture your child's spiritual development.

Take Time After School with Your Children

Save the first thirty minutes when your child gets home from school for them. Try not to be on the phone or working on a project. Meet them at the bus or at the door. Nothing makes a child feel more special than knowing we are happy to see them.

Use this time to go through their backpack, see their papers for the day, and review what homework they have for that night. Of course, on days when they have after-school activities, we wait until they are back home to go through the backpack and papers. I can't stress enough how important this time can be for saving time later. You'll prevent lost notes and assignments. You'll also know how much time your child should allot that day to getting homework done.

Use after-school time as a sharing and snack time together. My children seem to want to share their day with me when we are sitting together, unhurried, after school. One of my daughters likes this time so well that as soon as she comes through the door, she walks right over to our meeting place and sits down, ready to talk and go over everything. I wouldn't trade this time with them for anything.

We have only three times to connect with our school age children each day: before school, after school, and right before they go to bed. Try to organize your day so every minute with each child counts.

Take Time to Eat Together

Begin eating together when the children are young. It becomes a good habit you'll rely on during their hard teen years. Schedule dinner time like a business appointment, even if some family members protest. They'll thank you some day for trying to keep everyone together.

If the normal dinner hour is not a good time for everyone to eat together, try changing to a later time when everyone is home. If you can't eat together at dinner, try to be together at breakfast.

If you are never able to eat together, set aside one day or evening as family time. Don't let anything or anyone come in the way of this very special time. Turn off the television. That dinner/family time is more important than anything else.

Have a family rule that once you've served everyone and sat down, you don't get back up from the table until dinner is over. I used to hop up and down during a meal getting food or drinks for everyone. Children can learn to wait or get what they want themselves.

Try eating out occasionally, even with toddlers. No, I am not kidding! I look for creative ways to handle going out because children love it and eating out is a great way to celebrate special occasions. We even celebrate half-birthdays. If you have toddlers or very active young children, plan to dine at off-peak hours. Order as soon as you sit down and ask that the children's meals be brought out first. You can always walk around the restaurant or lobby until the food comes.

Take Time for Activities with Your Children

Celebrate often with small activities. Even a trip for an ice cream treat can be a celebration for something special. It's time together with just Mommy. Make every day special for your children by thinking up and telling them one good thing about that day. Monday might be special because Daddy is in town. Friday may be special because it's family night. Life can be celebrated in little things every day. You will be focusing on the little windows of time we have with our children.

Put together scrapbooks for your children. Create your own, or use the scrapbook-making as an activity for the family. The important thing is to keep a record of your children's lives for them to have when they are grown. These works of art are examples of their childhood and wonderful reminders of their roots. When I think I can't do another page, I remember my mother, who created a scrapbook for each of her seven children. That's dedication!

If you need some help with making scrapbooks for your family, contact Creative Memories. This company has representatives who conduct workshops to show how to create scrapbooks. They have many beautiful books and wonderful ideas to show you. There are a variety of scrapbooks you can focus on:

- A photo scrapbook for all the pictures you take. When pictures come back from the film developer, mark the date, the names of the people, and places. Keep pictures on your desk (not in a drawer) until you can put them in a scrapbook.

- An individual photo scrapbook for each child. Each of my daughters has her own scrapbook with pictures that focus on her.

- A school scrapbook. Each of my girls has a preprinted book with pages for each grade. It has a folder for their special papers and report cards. They love to go back through and see how they used to write.

- A travel scrapbook. Each of our girls has one. I want them to remember all the trips we have taken together.

If this sounds like too much, it probably is! But, my children love their scrapbooks and appreciate the work I have done on them, so I am motivated to continue.

Save your children's art projects from different holidays in a bag, box or tray. When you decorate for that holiday, you can use the precious things they made when they were little. For example, each November I go down to the basement and pull out my Thanksgiving decorations. We decorate the table with construction paper turkeys, Pilgrims, and Indians my children have made through the years. One of my favorites is a cut-out turkey where my four-year-old daughter wrote what she was thankful for on each feather. She wrote the usual: food, family, etc. On the last feather, she wrote, "I'm thankful I go to the potty!"

When your children are involved in an activity such as soccer or ballet, attend as many of the games or recitals as you can. Children love to have their parents cheering them on and supporting them.

Remember to take time one-on-one with each of your children. A child has fun at an amusement park, but rocking in a chair together or playing a sport together brings them more fulfilling love. What children like best is your undivided attention.

Take Time to Help Your Child Succeed in School

No, I don't mean doing their homework. But you can help them develop good attitudes, as well as a routine.

Talk positively about school. The way your child perceives your feeling about school and teachers will have a direct effect on how he or she feels about them.

Be consistent with schedules. Children respond well to order. If you establish a firm pattern for school days and nights you will find yourself arguing less often about the little things. Let your children know the schedule, and the burden of responsibility will gradually shift from parent to child.

Designate a specific time slot for them to do their homework. This needs to be a time that works with their schedule and yours. Provide a place that is quiet with good light, work space, and supplies. Help them develop good study habits. Encourage them to tackle the hard projects first, to plan ahead for projects, and to know that it's their homework, not yours.

Put everything in its place. Designate a place for coats and backpacks, as well as a time for you to go over their assignments and papers. The best time for this is when your children first get home. Value the work they show you and have a good attitude reviewing their work. Praise before you offer advice. Have a place designated for long-term projects that won't be disturbed while the project is being worked on.

Go to Parent/Teacher conferences. Get to know your children's teachers. Help in the classroom as often as you can. Statistics show that the children with the highest grades and the fewest discipline problems are those whose parents are involved with their education.

Help them get enough rest. The best tonic for sluggish mornings begins the night before. Establish a firm bedtime routine and stick to it. This is hard for working parents because they want to spend more time with their children, or feel guilty that they don't. But children need to be alert to learn. Some teenagers have after-school jobs keeping them up too late. Help your teenager balance the time between job and school work. Understand that some teens need more time for homework and sleep and can't keep up with a job, too.

Expect the best from your children. When our expectations are high, children have a solid goal to reach for. However, be realistic with their abilities. Not every child can make straight *A*s. Discuss with your children's teachers their capabilities. Don't punish your children for getting *B*s and *C*s if this is their best.

Remember that times have changed in the public school system. In the 1940s the top problems reported by teachers were such items as talking, chewing gum, and running in the halls. A similar study in the 1990s showed the top problems to be drug and alcohol abuse, pregnancy, rape, suicide, and assault. (Sources: Fullerton, California Police Department and the California Department of Education). Now more than ever, we need to need to know what is going on in our children's lives and at their schools. We need to teach and show our children moral values. We need to teach them how to survive morally in today's world. These are too important to leave for others to do.

Take Time to Discipline and Train Your Children

"Train up a child in the way he should go, even when he is old he will not depart from it" (Prov. 22:6). Parents play a large role in laying the foundation for future spiritual growth and understanding. Though the challenges are many, the process is not that complex. You know how God's love changes your life. The more you communicate and model God's love for your children, the more they will grasp deeper spiritual concepts later on. As we show love to our children, it will be easier to discipline them because we'll already relate with them on a deep and sincere level.

Dr. Gary Chapman and Dr. Ross Campbell explain this process in their book *The Five Love Languages of Children*:

> Every child has an emotional tank, a place of emotional strength that can fuel him through the challenging days of childhood and adolescence. We need to fill our children's emotional tanks with unconditional love, because real love is always unconditional. Only unconditional love can prevent problems such as resentment, feelings of being unloved, guilt, fear, and insecurity. Only as we give our children this love will we be able to deeply understand them and deal with their behaviors, good or bad.

Teach your children the Ten Commandments (Exod. 20:1–17). Disciplining our children goes together with training our children. It is a constant, daily activity, totally centered on our love for them. Unfortunately, with the growing collapse of the moral environment we live in today, it is harder to discipline and train our children.

Expect your children to obey. Never forget who is the parent and who is the child. Nothing is as sad to see as a family where the children are in charge. A family is not a democracy. The parents are to have the final say or everyone is in trouble. It is important to have guidelines that lead to this Christian obedience we expect of our children. In *Dr. Dobson Answers Your Questions,* Dr. James Dobson gives valuable tips toward this:

- Define the boundaries before you enforce them. Use common sense and make sure your child knows what you expect as far as manners, respect, and the Golden Rule.

- Explain your expectations to your children. If you know you will be driving in heavy traffic a long way, explain to your children that you need their help by being quiet and not fighting. Children respond well when we share with them what we need from them.

- If your child defies or challenges you, respond clearly and decisively. It's important to be confident when you face a nose-to-nose confrontation with your child.

- Know the difference between willful defiance and ordinary childish irresponsibility. If your child forgets to feed the dog or make his bed, remember that these behaviors are typical of childhood. If the behavior continues, then you can decide necessary consequences.

- After a confrontation is over, be sure that your child feels loved and reassured. By all means, open your arms and let him come. Hold him close and tell him of your love. Let him know again why he was punished and how he can avoid the trouble next time.

- Avoid impossible demands. Never punish him for wetting the bed involuntarily or for not becoming potty trained by one year of age or for doing poorly in school when he is trying hard.

- Let love be your guide. If there is genuine love, affection, and respect in your relationship with your child, things will work out, despite some parental mistakes and errors.

Never tell your child he is bad. It is only his behavior that is bad.

Treat each child as an individual. Don't favor one child over another. Don't label children by saying things like, "She's the artist in the family," or "He's the family athlete." This creates disharmony. Let your children know there is room in the family for two children to excel at the same thing.

Encourage your children to work out their own disagreements. This eases rivalry and teaches kids how to negotiate. Just say, "You have to figure this problem out yourselves. You're smart. You can do it!"

Let all your children, even the youngest, give opinions for making decisions. Every member of the family should be respected for their preferences. But remind them that Mom and Dad will make the final decisions.

Don't buy your children every toy. Provide creative toys such as paints, crayons and blank paper. Let them build their own toys in the backyard or playroom. Their play during these early years is really hard work and they are forming great imaginations and work ethics when they play and create.

Teach your children manners. Not just manners at the dinner table, but manners about being kind, giving compliments, team-playing, and making tiny sacrifices. Learning to write thank-you notes and responding graciously when others do kind things for them are important in the overall development of a child. As Judith Martin says, "A polite child grows up to get the friends and the dates and the job interviews because people respond to good manners. It's the language of all human behavior."

Turn off the television! When it is on, monitor what is seen and how much time it is used. This goes for videos too. I've seen mothers distract their young children with Disney videos for hours because it makes mom's life easier, and they feel the videos are better for their children than regular television programming. But the children are still sitting, watching like zombies. Let their little minds grow and develop and learn. Television watching inhibits initiative, curiosity, motivation, imagination, reasoning, and attention span. While they are watching, not one skill is being exercised.

Take Time to Teach Your Children Scheduling

The best part of being organized is that many areas of our life will flow more freely with more available time for ourselves and others. As my life gets more organized, I am able to be an example for my children in how to organize theirs. Having schedules and plans are extremely important in helping your children become more independent and responsible.

Expect them to help with housework. Children should be contributing members of their families.

- Post a schedule of chores for your children in your kitchen. You can even buy a large chart printed for this purpose. We have one already divided up into different chores with stars that will stick on it.

- Get your children in the habit of checking off each chore they do. Some chores are worth money. At the end of the week, have them count up what they are owed. For chores you really want them to do, such as practicing the piano, assign more money. This one tip has taken the responsibility of chores off me and put it onto the children. Our girls can't wait to do their chores so they can mark them off, knowing at the end of the week they will see a reward.

- Have some chores that must be done without pay. Kids should help around the house because they are part of a family, not solely because they get money. But since we live in a world that rewards hard work with pay, our children need to learn this concept, too. They also need to learn how to handle their money. Chores provide a sense of accomplishment, enlarging a child's feelings of worth. And learning how to do different chores will equip your children to live with roommates and spouses.

• Remember when we tell our children to clean their rooms, our definition of that task and theirs differ. Part of training our children is to invest time and effort into teaching them how to organize and clean. Habits of cleanliness do not develop automatically with age. Children need neatness training. Show them how to fold sweaters, hang pants, organize drawers. Provide special files for homework papers and projects. Children tend to keep the habits they build in childhood. Being able to organize belongings and storage space is a valuable skill they'll use all their lives.

Schedule your daily activities at a consistent time. Keep your dinner hour regular and early so that you will have the time to spend with your children in the evening. Also, avoid a giant rush by keeping breakfast and departure time the same each morning. Pray with your children each morning, or say, "God bless you today!" to them.

Have children lay out school clothes the night before. And make sure everyone agrees then! Don't argue the next morning about what they are wearing. Place bookbags, papers, lunches, notes to teachers, etc., by the door so nothing will be left behind.

Keep a calendar of the family's activities posted in a place that is convenient for all to see. A magnetic calendar that attaches to the refrigerator is useful. Your children can help you schedule their activities by writing them on this calendar. It is a great tool for making sure everyone knows where everyone else is.

Keep a "no television" rule on school nights. Right after dinner, you can start getting your youngest child ready for bed and reading without the fight to see television. As you finish with that child, you are ready for the next one. Does this take all night? Yes. I made the choice to be with my children instead of watching television when they were toddlers. I admit it was hard. But television will always be around, while children grow up all too quickly. Organizing your home and building quality relationships with the people you love takes sacrifice, but the end results are priceless. The "no television" rule should apply also to your older children. They need a quiet house for homework, chores, activities, and reading.

Find out how long it takes to get your preschoolers dressed for bed or for their day or for other activities that impose a time limit. Then allow them more time so you don't have to say "hurry up" so often. If your teenager is always late, tell him the time you will be leaving and make him responsible. If it's time to go and he isn't ready, leave without him or allow him to suffer some other consequence. This keeps you from nagging and teaches time-management.

Don't forget to delegate to your children, especially as they get older. I remember my twelve-year-old daughter waiting for her lunch one summer day. I suddenly realized she was old enough to make her lunch and the family's, and she became a big help for me. Sometimes I catch myself doing chores that could be delegated to members of the family, but one of our main goals as mothers is to teach our children how to live on their own. So, delegate. Teach them to get organized. You can begin teaching your children at age four or five. They can make their beds, put away their clothes and toys, set and clear the table, and dust with a feather duster, which most love to do. Remember, young children love to help and make you proud.

Raising children can be difficult, and at times I wonder if I am doing anything right. I want to have my life balanced and organized well enough so that my children get my very best. In fact, the main purpose of a more organized life is to have time for your family.

Twenty Ways to Make Your Children Feel Great!

1. **Show unconditional love.** This means you truly love the inside of your child—who they are, not what they do.

2. **Be careful with your anger.** Don't discipline in anger. If you are out of control, you or the child should immediately go to another room until you cool off. Do not yell unless the house is on fire.

3. **Make requests and instructions clear.** Have younger children repeat what you have just said so everyone is in agreement.

4. **Learn to listen.** Become a great listener for your child even at those times when you don't want to.

5. **Take your child's feelings seriously.** Kids remember little of what we tell them, but they never forget how we make them feel.

6. **Appreciate who your child is.** A child is a gift from God, the richest of all blessings. Find one thing about them to appreciate daily.

7. **Discipline your child with firmness and reason.** If he knows you are fair, you will not lose his respect or his love. Make sure the punishment you give fits the "crime." Taking the time and effort to discipline and direct your child shows you care. This makes him feel secure.

8. **Spend time alone with each child daily.** Read to them and listen to them talk about their day.

9. **Allow your child to do things for himself.** Help him become more independent—that is our goal in raising children. Teach them there is dignity in hard work and that a useful life is a rewarding life.

10. **Respect your child's possessions.** Never go through their mail or their diaries or listen in on phone conversations (if you suspect drugs or crime, talk with a professional).

11. **Respect your child's opinions.** If you attack her when her viewpoint differs from yours, she will stop talking to you. The growing up years are when your child begins to form opinions. Be free to give your opinion and to live the life you preach; allow your child that same freedom.

12. **Understand your child's abilities.** You might've been an Olympic swimmer but that doesn't mean your child will be. Encourage your

child to try many different activities so that as she reaches adulthood, she understands her strengths and interests. Don't push her into something that only you want her to do. She has her own life.

13. **When possible, respect your children's choices.** You may have to step in when their choices involve friends you don't approve of. But try to respect their choices in clothes, music, etc. Interfere only when a choice endangers the child's welfare.

14. **Teach your child to value the health of his body.** Teach at an early age the dangers of drugs, especially alcohol, smoking, and sexual sins, and continue talking to your older children about these dangers.

15. **Do not let your child put himself down.** Encourage him. Build him up. Remind him that each person on earth is here for a special reason and purpose and he is unique in the eyes of God and of you.

16. **Verbally say "I love you" every day.** Other ways to communicate love: a hug, a back rub, rumpling your child's hair, a kiss, letting your child sit in your lap, and spending quality one-on-one time with her.

17. **Speak to your child at eye level** and let your body language show you are available to her.

18. **Avoid double standards and mixed messages.** Don't show favoritism. Never compare him with others who may have preformed better.

19. **Be mature enough to share your feelings and admit when you are wrong.** Always tell your child you are sorry after a disagreement.

20. **Teach your child to love God and others.** Take him to a place of worship and be an example. Faith in God can be your child's strength and light when all else fails.

(With thanks to Zionsville Newsletter)

Lo, children are a heritage of the LORD; and the fruit of the womb is his reward. As arrows are in the hand of a mighty man, so are children of the youth. Happy is the man that hath his quiver full of them.   —Psalm 127:3–5 KJV

Bringing Home Chapter 9

She opens her mouth in wisdom,
And the teaching of kindness is on her tongue.
—Proverbs 31:26

As a mother, you need to teach and lead your children with great love and kindness, and you need God's wisdom and strength in order to do this. As you take each step toward becoming a more organized woman, organize the areas of your children's lives which will result in an organized and flowing home life.

DISCUSSION QUESTIONS

1. What does the Bible say about the importance of children?
2. What activities do you currently do with your children? What would you like to do more of?
3. Why is spiritual nurture often viewed as less important than social and physical nurture?
4. What are some ways you make your children feel more special?
5. How could you help your child become a better student?
6. Are you happy with the discipline and training that you give your children? What could you change or add?

PERSONAL APPLICATION

- Pick at least three things you could do for or with your children this week to show you think they're great . . . and do the first one today!

10

CHANGE YOUR HOUSE

INTO A HOME

She looks well to the ways of her household,
And does not eat the bread of idleness.
—Proverbs 31:27

HANGING YOUR HOUSE into a home can be one of the most fulfilling goals a woman can have. Even if you are not the type of person who likes to clean, you probably love the warm feeling you get when you welcome your family and friends to your home. Just think about Christmas. Imagine a tree all aglow with bright lights, and presents overflowing near a roaring fire in the fireplace. The fire casts a golden haze of light on the windows revealing snowflakes floating down. The smell of fresh baked breads and cookies drift in from the kitchen.

Yes, when my home is full of good food, beautiful decorations, and loved ones, I have a true sense of contentment and fulfillment. My goal is to have this same holiday contentment in my home every day. It takes work, time, effort, and even wisdom. Our homes are built by understanding how to keep a house in functioning order and how to keep the people inside together and united.

Titus 2:5 encourages us to be "sensible, pure, workers at home." This verse can be an encouragement for us because it reveals one of the goals the Lord has for us as wives and homemakers: being hard workers in our homes. In fact, the psalmist says "Unless the LORD builds the house, they labor in vain who build it" (Ps. 127:1). In other words, we need to put the Lord in our life and in our home-building. If we follow his guidelines, we will succeed with this goal.

Jesus mentions in John 14:2 that he has a house for us: "In My Father's house are many dwelling places; if it were not so, I would have told you; for I go to prepare a place for you." How exciting! Jesus is actually preparing a place for you and me in God's house, which is heaven. We will soon see his house, but would you invite him to yours? You would probably want Jesus to see your house at its best. And I know Jesus will make your home in heaven its best because of his great love for all of us.

So also, we should keep our homes clean and in order for our loved ones. The Proverbs 31 woman looked well to the ways of her household. She would have to be organized to do so. And as verse 27 says, she wasn't idle or lazy. She knew she had a great purpose by taking care of her household and doing her very best.

Just as the Proverbs woman did, you too can "look well to the ways of your household." I know keeping a house is difficult, especially when there are children to take care of. Though there are many helpful tips here, remember that the best tip is you! Just get up and do the very best you can every day, asking yourself, "What kind of home will I build today?"

Organize Your Home

Remember that organizing reduces stress. Reduced stress means more joy and peace in your life.

First, walk through your house and determine what room should be organized first, second, and so on. Make a list of these rooms and promise yourself you will give each room one week. It may not take this long, but by giving yourself a week, you make a commitment to get it done thoroughly.

As you go through your house room by room, *consider which of these four things you will do with every item in that room:*

- Keep it if you use it.
- Give it away if you don't.
- Sell it in a garage sale or to a friend.
- Throw it away!

We have too much stuff cluttering our homes. The more we have, the more we are responsible for.

As you go from room to room, *list how you could organize, decorate or clean that room better.* Organizing isn't just putting in order. It's also developing your house into your particular style of home. If you have a budget for it, ask a home decorator to visit your home and help with ideas. Many furniture stores offer this service for free.

List smaller areas, such as closets or the laundry room, that need reorganizing. Try scheduling one a week until they are all finished.

Determine to stay on top of rooms that continue to get disorganized. Concentrate most of your time on these rooms. For me, the kitchen and the master bathroom are the hardest areas to keep orderly and clean. I have had to adjust my expectations and just clean them as consistently as I can.

When organizing your kitchen, you might want to clean out the cabinets and drawers, clean the shelves and add fresh shelf paper. Perhaps you need to rearrange some cabinets. Periodically, I clean out my cabinets and pantry, removing unused, outdated foods. (For more tips on kitchen organization, see chapter 2.)

When you move into a new home, use these same tips. With paper and pen, walk through each room of the house and decide which room should be unpacked first. Leave the boxes in the other rooms and don't worry about them.

- If you have to sleep in the new house the first night, pack one box with sheets for the beds, the coffee pot, and towels and tissue for the bathroom so the necessities can be unpacked first.

- Unpack the kitchen first, bathrooms next, then bedrooms.

- List which rooms need shelves, drapes, blinds, and so on. By placing these needs and wants on a list, you can decide what should be done first, and you won't be overwhelmed.

Clean Effectively

There are hundreds of books on cleaning. The best tip I can give you is that cleaning a house can be simple and does not need to take all day. But it does take organization! Staying organized will keep your home cleaner and in order day by day.

Decide on a weekly cleaning plan. I have a two-story house. Once a week, I clean the downstairs at night (vacuum, mop kitchen floor, dust, and clean the half-bath). The next morning, I do the upstairs and am usually finished by noon. My family helps, so I can't take all the credit. When my husband is in town, he vacuums. The girls help dust and clean their bathrooms.

Devise a quick way to do necessary daily cleaning. I straighten the downstairs before I go to bed at night (unload the dishwasher, take out the newspaper, adjust pillows on the sofa). The next morning I straighten the upstairs (wipe down bathroom counters, make beds, take trash and dirty clothes downstairs). I call this morning routine my "five-minute quick clean." I recommend one every morning. If a house is quick-cleaned daily, then the once-a-week heavy cleaning won't take nearly as long. Your own quick-clean may sometimes take longer than five minutes, but it will still be a big help to you.

To quick-clean simply means to quickly put your house in order daily. Wipe kitchen and bathroom counters, take down dirty towels and add fresh ones, empty trash cans, empty dirty clothes hampers, and make beds. Check children's rooms for dirty clothes, and for curling irons, lights, and radios left on. Begin a load of laundry, sweep the kitchen floor, and load the dishwasher. In less than forty-five minutes, your house is set for the day. (I have a cordless telephone, so to save time I work while talking on the phone. In fact, I usually do something around the house while on the phone.)

Remember that clutter is what makes a house look messy. In fact, 40 percent of cleaning a house is getting rid of clutter. Clutter causes stress. Remove as much clutter as you can before you begin to clean. You will be able to clean much faster. And don't be afraid to throw out or give this stuff away.

Sweep once a day, either after breakfast or after you have done the dinner dishes. This will keep the rest of the house cleaner because crumbs and dirt won't get tracked through the house.

Every day, clean your counters in the kitchen and bathroom with a specific product for that purpose. It only takes a few seconds, but they will look wonderful and will be germ free. Use rubber gloves when you clean. You won't mind cleaning nearly as much.

Have cleaning supplies in every bathroom, or put your cleaning supplies in a bucket and carry it with you to all the bathrooms. Keep a roll of paper towels and a spray cleaner under each sink so everyone can help with cleaning counters. To keep the showers clean, keep a spray bottle of cleaner (I use Clean Shower) in the shower. Whoever uses the shower sprays the walls, doors and floor upon exiting.

Schedule your major cleaning for the same day each week. Your house will stay neat with consistency. This is how women cleaned many years ago. Each day of the week was designated for one particular task: Monday was usually wash day, Tuesday was baking day, etc.

Use the old fashioned "spring cleaning" for big jobs in your house such as windows, carpets, and washing blankets. If you know you will have a specific time each year to do these harder jobs, you won't worry about them the rest of the year.

If your children won't pick up their shoes or toys, each day throw them into a plastic bin or box and charge them twenty-five cents to get items back. This teaches children their clutter is their responsibility, not yours.

Put a folded towel or rug by the doors leading to the outside and make everyone wipe their feet each time they come into the house. I have discovered that this is the best way to keep shoes clean and the rest of your house free from dirt and dust. You will also be protecting your carpets and helping them last longer.

Eat meals and snacks in your kitchen or dining room. This will keep your sofas, chairs, and carpets much cleaner and save you hours of cleaning time and money. For the television room, keep popcorn on hand. Air-popped popcorn isn't messy and is great when watching movies.

Measure how much time a particular job takes to do. For example, I don't like to fold clothes. So, I timed it once and discovered one large load of white clothes took ten minutes to fold. That isn't very long. Now that I know that, I don't mind folding clothes as much.

Give yourself time limits for each job, with a prize at the end. For example, if I can clean my upstairs by eleven, I stop and take my walk or read the newspaper. I find I always work better and faster if there is something I want to do when I am finished.

As you begin to organize your home, remember what the goal is. The goal is taking small steps in different areas that result in the large step of becoming more organized. One area might be taking the time to clean your home better. Other areas could be reducing clutter, managing your time and home, or just making the effort every morning in getting the house in shape. It does take work to have a home well managed but the end result is less stress and more time for you and the family you love. With God's help, you can do it.

Create a Peaceful Home

Do you want a godly home? A home that is governed by God and run with efficiency and order? Then think about these suggestions from *A Godly Home* by Joyce Meyer:

Speak in vocal tones that bring peace. Avoid screaming and yelling; avoid being harsh.

Build each other up. Don't tear each other down. Don't criticize. Be positive, not negative.

Work together to keep order. Teach your children to pick up after themselves.

Laugh! Laughter is medicine to your soul. Have fun together often and regularly.

Be slow to anger, slow to speak, quick to hear. Be a good listener. Forgive each other. Have mercy for other's faults. God certainly has forgiven us so we should forgive others.

Don't be overly sensitive. Often family members say things that hurt us, without intending any harm.

Do not judge. Each person in a family goes through different problems because of different ages, circumstances, health, and stress.

Don't say, "Hurry up!" all the time. This one phrase can steal such peace and joy. Organize your schedule so you have more time.

Don't worry. If your mind isn't peaceful, your unrest will infiltrate your life and home.

Make your house a member of the family. In other words, your house should be a home, a refuge from the world. It should be a place of warmth where family pictures are hung, where everyone contributes to its care, and where friends can visit (this thought is from *Seven Highly Effective Secrets for a Family* by Stephen R. Covey).

Remember that you are the guardian of your home. Keep your home full of the word of God and let your home and your life reflect his glory. Order is just another part in the design and decorating of your home. With a little more effort, your home will have your love and your personality all through it. And just as you are working and building up your home, so is the Lord building up you.

> You also, like living stones, are being built into a spiritual house for a holy priesthood, to offer up spiritual sacrifices acceptable to God through Jesus Christ.   —1 Peter 2:5

Bringing Home Chapter 10

She looks well to the ways of her household,
And does not eat the bread of idleness.
—Proverbs 31:27

Women tell me that maintaining their homes is their biggest struggle in being organized. But with a few helpful tips and some motivation, anyone can develop a more organized home, permeated with a godly flavor.

DISCUSSION QUESTIONS

1. Do you want your house to be a home? If so, what are some ways you could accomplish this?
2. Now might be a good time to walk through your home (either visually or physically) and decide how you could organize, decorate or clean each room in order to make your house a home. Write down your ideas and then begin taking action.
3. How could you implement the "five-minute quick-clean" to your mornings? What would be a good day, each week, to do your heavy cleaning?
4. Clutter is the enemy of an organized home. What clutter could you get rid of in your home?
5. Think how businesses organize and schedule things. What are some ways you could organize and schedule the house responsibilities better?

PERSONAL APPLICATION

- What are the overall goals you have for your home? Take time to think this through, then write these goals down.
- On a sheet of paper, map out the different rooms in your home. In each room, write goals of what you want to accomplish for that room.

Her children rise up and bless her;
Her husband also, and he praises her, saying:
"Many daughters have done nobly,
But you excel them all."

—Proverbs 31:28–29

REMEMBER IN THE BEGINNING of the book when I talked about how ambitious we must be in our journey to becoming an organized woman? So far we've journeyed through ten chapters of hard work, learning to organize all the different areas of our lives so that we might live more fully the lives God has called us to. We've been learning how to be better wives, how to manage our shopping and cooking and how to schedule our days. We've learned how to make our job and home life work together, as well as our health and strength and work load. We've worked on our closets and on being more creative. We've worked on prioritizing our relationships as we reach out to our families and to others in need. And we have learned how to turn a house into our home.

Now we come to step 11 and the beautiful Proverbs verses listed above. Just as God rested on the seventh day from all his labor in the creation of the world, we Proverbs women now come to these verses, a place to rest and replenish ourselves.

How wonderful praise is. Every time I read these two verses, my heart soars. What a blessing to hear our husbands and children honor us with their hearts and the words of their mouths in this way.

Because of the love, time, and commitment the Proverbs woman has put into the running of her household, she now receives the fruit of her labors: her family's love, admiration and praise. When a husband tells his wife she is the best, then all her sacrifices have been worth it.

But even as we rest, receiving deserved praise from our family, our journey continues. We can't stay at this resting place. We continue to serve our families, friends, and the others God puts into our lives. To do this, we turn our attention to being restored, so that we will have the energy to go on: "Let us not lose heart in doing good, for in due time we shall reap if we do not grow weary" (Gal. 6:9).

It's time now to take another step, a step towards freeing ourselves within, making our inner selves ready to receive the praise God wants us to have. If we are fully restored emotionally, physically, and spiritually, then we can fully receive. Once we are free of addictions, of past hurts, of unforgiveness, we can become whole.

Philippians 4:6–9 is a passage of scripture that can minister to your soul. The Apostle Paul wrote this while in jail, yet it is full of joy and peace:

> Be anxious for nothing, but in everything by prayer and supplication with thanksgiving let your requests be made known to God. And the peace of God, which surpasses all comprehension, will guard your hearts and your minds in Christ Jesus. Finally, brethren, whatever is true, whatever is honorable, whatever is right, whatever is pure, whatever is lovely, whatever is of good repute, if there is any excellence and if anything worthy of praise, dwell on these things. The things you have learned and received and heard and seen in me, practice these things, and the God of peace will be with you.

Here are some tips for restoring ourselves.

Restore Yourself Physically

For some suggestions on restoring yourself physically, turn back to chapter 5, "Get in Shape." In addition here are two bonus tips:

Take time every day for yourself: perhaps take a walk, soak in a bubble bath, or read by the fireplace. Even if it is for only fifteen minutes, you will feel like a new person and can give to others.

Seek peace in your life. Put forth the effort to organize your life so that the end result is peace. And remember that peace isn't the absence of problems, it's the ability to deal with them.

Restore Yourself Emotionally

Be content with what you have in your life. It is fine to dream of something new, but until it comes, be content now. As Paul said in Philippians 4:11, "I have learned to be content in whatever circumstances I am."

Restore yourself by having kindness, compassion and generosity for others. Be true to yourself and to others. Be authentic. Have an ease about yourself of truth and honesty. Reject hostility towards others. Work at your relationships. Take care of friendships. Hold close people you love.

Have a spirit of joy. Joy doesn't come from circumstances. Circumstances change daily. Joy comes from the inside. Cultivate a true joy of life inside yourself. It takes an act of the will to focus on the good, but as time goes by, this spirit of joy will come naturally.

Restore Yourself Spiritually

Put God first in your life. Ask him to direct you daily. Only God can fully restore you. As you "seek first His kingdom and His righteousness" all those things you need in our life "will be added to you" (Matt. 6:33).

Be a woman of character. Fill your mind and life with thoughts and actions that honor Christ—he actually is with you in everything you do.

Have a thankful heart. Give thanks to God daily along with giving thanks to your husband and children for all they do. Even if you can only think of one thing, express appreciation for that one thing.

Expect great things! Anticipate the plans God has for you. Be ready to serve the Lord every day, putting him and your prayer life first, and you will be refreshed.

Praise God every day. This is most powerful of all. What happens when we praise God? According to Dr. Charles Stanley's *In Touch Magazine*:

- Praise magnifies God. Praise puts our focus on God, not our problems. Our thinking is wrapped in God's power, presence, and ability.

- Praise humbles us. When we worship God, we gain a right view of ourselves. Excess pride and ego are deflated. We have a healthy self-image based on God's view of who we are. By removing pride, praise strengthens us against temptation.

- Praise reveals our devotion to Christ. If we love Christ, we will praise him. If he has first place in our life, we will honor him with worship and thanksgiving.

- Praise motivates us to holy living. Praise opens our hearts to want to live the way God desires —holy and separated unto him, to do his will above our own, to want to be like him more than anyone else. The more we worship him, the more like him we will become.

- Praise ministers to three aspects of our life. Praise ministers to our spirit by creating humility and releasing joy. Praise ministers to our inner self by clearing our mind, calming our emotions, and setting our will. Praise ministers to our physical body by releasing tension and stress and replacing it with God's supernatural energy.

May you be restored, ready to receive the praise and blessings from your loved ones.

This is what the Sovereign LORD, the Holy One of Israel, says: "In repentance and rest is your salvation, in quietness and trust is your strength." —Isaiah 30:15 NIV

Bringing Home Chapter 11

Her children rise up and bless her;
Her husband also, and he praises her, saying:
"Many daughters have done nobly,
But you excel them all."

—Proverbs 31:28–29

Because of the love, time, and commitment this woman has put into the running of her household, she now reaps the rewards from her family: their love, admiration and praise. When a husband tells his wife she is the best of all other women, then all her sacrifices have been worthwhile.

DISCUSSION QUESTIONS

1. What changes could you make in your life so that your family will "rise up and praise" you?
2. How can you take care of the needs of your family and yourself?
3. Review and discuss the tips on restoring ourselves. How could you use them in your life?

PERSONAL APPLICATION

- Review how much love, time and commitment you've put into becoming a Proverbs 31 woman. What areas would you improve upon? What areas are you pleased with?

Charm is deceitful and beauty is vain,
But a woman who fears the LORD,
* she shall be praised.*
Give her the product of her hands,
And let her works praise her in the gates.
                              —Proverbs 31:30–31

EVERYONE HAS a basic need for approval and admiration. People try different things to get this approval either from work, from relationships, from outward appearance, or from material acquisitions.

As women, we all want to be beautiful. We also want to be loved and praised. As we conclude Proverbs 31 with these last two verses, we see that though we desire charm and beauty, they are deceitful. That's because God created us to have an inner beauty that reflects his character.

The inner beauty of a woman and the way she conducts her life becomes her real beauty. Charm can be deceitful. To allow your outer beauty to be the most important thing in your life is vanity.

So where does the Proverbs 31 woman obtain her beauty, wisdom and ability to be all that she is trying to be? If, as the Bible says, charm is deceitful and beauty is vain, what can a woman do to be acknowledged and praised? Well, as the verse above says, she must fear the Lord. Proverbs 1:7 says, "The fear of the LORD is the beginning of knowledge." Women who desire to be all that the Lord wants them to be in this life must first have a fear (or knowledge) of who God is and who he wants to be in their life.

Wanting to have God in our life is the last step of our twelve steps to becoming a more organized woman. Turning to God for the strength and wisdom we need to keep our lives flowing is the best and wisest decision any woman can make.

Once you know that you want and need God in your life, the next step is to give your life to him. He promises he will come into your life through his Spirit. How can this be done?

First, acknowledge that you are a sinner. The Bible says, "For all have sinned and fall short of the glory of God" (Rom. 3:23). This verse means every single person has committed sins, making each a sinner. It is hard to acknowledge this truth, but it is true. From the time we are small, we want our own way, rather than God's way. Just watch a two-year-old rebelliously tell his mother, "No!" The Ten Commandments were given to us as laws to follow but also to show us that it is humanly impossible to keep every one. We cannot keep them, so they reveal to us that we are sinners. God sent his Son, Jesus Christ, to show us another way to him apart from the Law.

Second, understand that the penalty for being a sinner is death: "For the wages of sin is death [an eternal separation from God], but the free gift of God is eternal life in Christ Jesus our Lord" (Rom. 6:23). Our sins cause a separation between a Holy God and us: "But your iniquities [sins] have made a separation between you and your God, and your sins have hidden His face from you so that he does not hear" (Isa. 59:2). Since we are separated from God because of our sins, God sent his Son, Jesus Christ to restore us to him.

Our sins also cause a separation between people. Because of our sinful nature, relationships break. Bringing Jesus into our lives to take our sins away and restore us to God will also open our hearts for restoration to our husbands, our children, and our extended family. This is an important step for our lives as wives and mothers.

Third, realize that God is a God of great love. His desire is to have a loving relationship with us: "For God so loved the world, that He gave His only begotten Son, that whoever believes in Him should not perish, but have eternal life" (John 3:16). God had a great plan to bring you and me to him. God substituted Christ's perfection and purity for our imperfection and sin through Christ's death, burial, and resurrection: "For Christ died for sins once for all, the righteous for the unrighteous, to bring you to God. He was put to death in the body but made alive by the Spirit" (1 Peter 3:18). Jesus took away our sins, brought us back into a relationship with God, and he gave us a free gift of eternal life. Personally, I couldn't bear to live this life not knowing if I would ever see my family again after I die. I am amazed that some women will not talk about whether or not they will be going to heaven. But how could anyone not want to know for sure? The Bible says clearly that if we believe in him we will not die, but will have eternal life. Because of Jesus, I will see my family again!

Fourth, know that he gave us the right to become one of his children: "But as many as received Him, to them He gave the right to become the children of God, to those who believe in His name" (John 1:12). We actually are heirs to everything that is God's! And what a comforting thought to any woman who never had a father or never had a good relationship with her father. God says he will be the father to the fatherless. He wants to hold you in the "hollow of his hands" (Isa. 40:12) What a wonderful thought!

Fifth, Jesus is standing at the door to your heart, waiting for you to ask him in. "Behold I stand at the door and knock; if anyone hears My voice and opens the door, I will come in to him, and will dine with him, and he with Me" (Rev. 3:20). This is a great promise God gives to us. If you have never opened the door for Jesus to come into your life, then pray and ask Jesus to come into your life right now. Or, if you asked him years ago and are now ready to recommit your life to him, now is the time to right yourself before the Lord. This is such an important step because he can guide you and give you the strength you need in living every day.

To live the life of the Proverbs 31 woman, to live the Christian life, to be a loving wife and mother who can really make a difference in the lives of her family, you must have supernatural strength and help from God. Because we are all sinners, the only way to live a life that is full of love, joy, peace, patience, kindness, goodness, faithfulness, gentleness and self-control is to live a life that is controlled by God's Spirit. And his Spirit comes into our lives when we ask Jesus into our life. Only by his Holy Spirit can any of us live a godly life. We cannot do it by ourselves.

Making ourselves beautiful just on the outside is deceitful and vain. Making ourselves beautiful on the inside, by growing as God's children, shapes us into godly women, whose families will praise us.

Ask yourself if you have ever really given your whole heart and soul and life to the Lord. Confess your sins to him and then just ask him to take over your life and be your God: "If you confess with your mouth Jesus is Lord, and believe in your heart that God raised Him from the dead, you shall be saved; for with the heart a person believes, resulting in righteousness, and with the mouth he confesses, resulting in salvation" (Rom. 10:9–10). Once you have asked the Lord Jesus into your life, you then have his Spirit living within you to guide you, direct you, and give you supernatural strength. Only with his strength can we live the Christian life.

God can also take away any guilt about the past and can make you brand new inside: "Therefore if anyone is in Christ, he is a new creature; the old things passed away; behold, new things have come" (2 Cor. 5:17). When this guilt is lifted by God, you will have new strength, new hope, new abilities to manage and cope with your life. This is such a blessing! Once you have given your life to the Lord, here are some tips to help you grow.

Find the Right Church

It's important for you to have fellowship with other believers. Find a church where the Bible is taught and where your children will learn and grow through Sunday School and other programs.

Look for a church close to your home. If your church is nearby, you will want to spend more time there than if it is far away.

See if your church has a weekly Bible study where you could begin to learn about God's word and grow as a godly woman. If not, ask if they know of any neighborhood Bible studies. There are several good ones available nationwide:

- Stonecroft Ministries (Friendship Bible Coffees)
- Bible Study Fellowship
- Community Bible Study
- Kay Arthur's Precept upon Precept

Call information for the numbers, and ask for a study near you.

Plan for a Fruitful Prayer Time

Begin each day with prayer, asking God to help you be an organized and godly woman. Some women have time for only one-sentence prayers. But try to schedule time during the day when you can pray with the Lord and read his Bible. The way I did this was to make a place in my home where my Bible and devotionals are located. I go there the same time every day to read and pray. It doesn't have to be a fancy place. Mine is a quiet corner of my bathroom. What is important is to make a place and a time for your quiet time alone with your heavenly Father.

Buy a daily devotional book. Some of these daily readings will only take a few minutes but will help you to focus on God each day. Only through his strength can we accomplish anything. Philippians 4:13 promises us that "I can do all things through Him who strengthens me."

Ask God to give you a special love and attitude so that the climate of your home is positive, uplifting, and fun. You can choose whether your loved ones will feel loved or not. Give as much love out as you can.

Seek God's day-to-day wisdom. Just as you can go through your house room by room to see what needs to be organized and cleaned, so you should also go through the rooms in your heart, soul, and spirit seeking what should be organized and cleaned, and what needs to go or stay, ready for the Lord to live there.

The work and life of a wife and mother is not appreciated nearly as much as it should be in our society. Whether or not we are appreciated here on Earth, we will be rewarded in Heaven by God. Why not work toward hearing the Lord say, "Well done, good and faithful servant" (Matt. 25:23)?

May you put the Lord first in your life, love him with all your heart, all your soul, and all your might; and may his love pour through you to the many others he has given you in this life. I pray that the life of the Proverbs woman will be an example to you as you step towards becoming a more organized woman.

Praise her for the many fine things she does. These good deeds of hers shall bring her honor and recognition from even the leaders of the nations   —Proverbs 31:31 TLB

Bringing Home Chapter 12

Charm is deceitful and beauty is vain,
But a woman who fears the LORD,
    she shall be praised.
Give her the product of her hands,
And let her works praise her in the gates.
                                    —Proverbs 31:30–31

The inner beauty of a woman and the way she conducts her life becomes her *real* beauty. This inner beauty comes from her love and respect of the Lord. Having a relationship with the Lord will flow into all the other areas of life, and then you too will be praised.

DISCUSSION QUESTIONS

1. What is the real beauty of a woman?
2. What does it mean to "fear the Lord"?
3. Where does the strength to do it all come from?
4. Can God take away any guilt you might have from anything you might have done or not done? (see 2 Cor. 5:17).
5. What are the steps in asking God to be in your life?

PERSONAL APPLICATION

- If you want God to be in your life, then pray right now for him to forgive you of your sins and to come into your heart.
- If you have already asked God to be a part of your life, are you having a daily quiet time with him including prayer and Bible reading? Are you attending a church and having fellowship with other believers? These steps are vital for you to grow as a Christian. May God bless you as you grow.

ANE JORDAN, born and raised in Atlanta, Georgia, is a recording artist, author, actress, national speaker, and seminar leader. She studied Fashion Merchandising and Marketing at Auburn University and received a degree from DeKalb College in Atlanta. Lane graduated from Georgia State University with a Bachelor of Arts degree in Journalism and Broadcasting. She has served as the Associate Producer for the weekly television program *In Touch* with Dr. Charles Stanley.

Lane now lives in Colorado with her husband, Larry, and their two daughters, Christi and Grace. She teaches a weekly Bible study, sings on a worship team and in a church choir, and is a speaker and singer for Christian women's groups. She just finished her first musical recording project, titled *How Do I Live?* Lane leads seminars, retreats, and workshops on her book, *12 Steps to Becoming a More Organized Woman*, based on Proverbs 31.

Along with her love for writing and singing, Lane enjoys sports, especially tennis, golf, walking, and hiking. She also loves to read and enjoys all types of needlework.

If you are interested in having Lane Jordan speak to your church or organization for seminars, workshops, retreats, special events, or media appearances, you may contact her at:

L'Angel Ministries
70 Deerwood Drive
Littleton, CO 80127
(303) 979-6744
Lanepjor@aol.com